bite-size sales tips

practical ways to improve your sales performance

Neil Watson & Steve Hurst

KOGAN PAGE

The masculine pronoun has been used throughout this book. This stems from a desire to avoid ugly and cumbersome language, and no discrimination, prejudice or bias is intended

First Indian Edition 2002

Kogan Page India Private Limited
4325/3 Ansari Road
New Delhi 110 002.

ISBN 81-7554-191-1

Rs. 145

Published by Vinod Vasishtha for Kogan Page India Private Limited,
4325/3 Ansari Road, Daryaganj, New Delhi 110 002, and Printed at
Raj Press, New Delhi

Contents

KOGAN PAGE INDIA

PRICE LIST 2001-2002

QTY	ISBN	Title/Author/Binding/Year	Price Rs.
		101 WAYS SERIES	
	8175541431	101 Ways to Better Business Writing by Timothy RV Foster, PB, 2001	135.00
	8175541520	101 Ways to Better Communication by Elizabeth Tierney, PB, 2001	135.00
	8175541504	101 Ways to Boost Customer Satisfaction by Timothy RV Foster,PB, 2001	135.00
	8175541490	101 Ways to Clean Up Your Act by Dianna Booher, PB, 2001	135.00
	817554144X	101 Ways to Generate Great Ideas by Timothy RV Foster, PB, 2001	135.00
	8175541482	101 Ways to Get More Business by Timothy RV Foster, PB, 2001	135.00
	8175541512	101 Ways to Improve Business Performance by Donald Waters,PB, 2001	135.00
	8175541474	101 Ways to Increase Your Sales by Patrick Forsyth, PB, 2001	135.00
	8175541466	101 Ways to Make a Professional Impact by Eleri Sampson, PB, 2001	135.00
	8175541458	101 Ways to Motivate Yourself by Christine Ingham, PB, 2001	135.00
		HOW TO BE A BETTER...SERIES	
	817554077X	At Creativity by Geoffrey Petty, PB, 1998	125.00
	8175540796	At Giving Presentation by Michael Stevens, PB, 1998	125.00
	8175540850	At Writing Reports & Proposals by Patrick Forsyth, PB, 1998	125.00
	8175540761	Communicator by Sandy McMillan, PB, 1998	125.00
	8175541083	Customer Care by Timothy R V Foster, PB, 2000	135.00
	8175540788	Decision Maker by Alan Barker, PB, 1998	125.00
	8175541075	Delegation and Coaching by Tony Athenrton, PB, 2000	135.00
	817554080X	Interviewer by Margaret Dale, PB, 1998	125.00
	8175541059	Managing Change by David Hussey, PB, 2000	135.00
	8175541067	Meeting by Allan Barkar, PB, 2000	135.00
	8175540818	Motivating People by John Allan, PB, 1998	125.00
	8175540826	Negotiator by John Mattock & John Ehrenborg, PB, 1998	125.00
	8175540834	Problem Solver by Michael Stevens, PB, 1998	125.00
	8175540842	Project Manger by Trevor L. Young, PB, 1998	125.00
	8175540869	Teambuilder by Rupert Eales-White, PB, 1998	125.00
	8175540877	Time Manager by Jane Smith, PB, 1998	125.00

QTY	ISBN	Title/Author/Binding/year	Price Rs.
		INSTANT SERIES	
	8175541156	Instant Brain Power by Brian Clegg, PB, 2000	160.00
	8175541679	Instant Coaching by Paul Birch, PB, 2002	160.00
	8175541121	Instant Creativity by Brain Clegg and Paul Brich, PB, 2000	160.00
	8175541695	Instant Interviewing by Brian Clegg, PB, 2002	160.00
	8175541113	Instant Leadership by Paul Birch, PB, 2000	160.00
	8175541148	Instant Motivation by Brian Clegg, PB, 1999	160.00
	8175541687	Instant Negotiation by Brian Clegg, PB , 2002	160.00
	8175541229	Instant Stress Management by Brian Clegg, PB, 2000	160.00
	817554113X	Instant Teamwork by Brian Clegg and Paul Birch, PB, 2000	160.00
	8175541105	Instant Time Management by Paul Birch, PB, 2000	160.00
		PERSONAL DEVELOPMENT	
	8175541393	Boost Your Intelligence by Harry Alder, PB, 2000	195.00
	8175541164	Creating Confidence by Meribeth Bunch, PB, 2000	135.00
	8175541172	Know Yourself Achieve Your Goals Through Better Self Knowledge By Allen Balke, PB, 2000	135.00
	8175541180	Powerful Presentations by John Mattock, PB, 2000	110.00
	817554189X	Transform Yourself by Ros Taylor, PB New, 2002	165.00
		PROFESSIONAL PAPERBACKS	
	8175540885	Creating A World Class Organization 2nd Ed. by Bryan D Prescott, PB, 1999	175.00
	8175540907	Designing Organizations, 3rd Ed. by Philip Sadler, PB, 1999	175.00
	8175540893	Goal Directed Project Management, 2nd Ed., by S. Andersen, PB, 1999	175.00
	8175540958	Profitable Customers by Charles Wilson, PB, 1999	175.00
	8175540966	Target Setting and Goal Achievement by Richard Hale, PB, 1999	175.00
	817554094X	The Handbook of Project Management by Trevor Young, PB, 1999	175.00
	8175540923	The Marketing Plan, 2nd Ed., by John Westwood, PB, 1999	175.00
	8175540974	The Top Consultant by Calvert Markham, PB, 1999	175.00
	8175540915	Total Leadership by Jim Barrett, PB, 1999	175.00
	8175540931	Transform Your Management Style by Hilary Walmsley, PB, 1999	175.00
		QUEST TOOL BOX SERIES	
	8175541040	Be Your Best by Steve Smith, PB, 1999	135.00
	8175541016	Build That Team by Steve Smith, PB, 1999	135.00
	8175541032	Create That Change by Steve Smith, PB, 1999	135.00
	8175541024	Make Things Happen by Steve Smith, PB, 1999	135.00
	8175541008	Solve That Problem by Steve Smith, PB, 1999	135.00

QTY	ISBN	Title/Author/Binding/year	Price Rs.
		RICHARD DENNY BEST SELLERS	
	817554192X	Communicate to Win by Richard Denny, PB, 2002	195.00
	8175541571	Motivate to Win by Richard Denny, PB, 2002	195.00
	8175541555	Selling to Win by Richard Denny, PB, 2002	195.00
	8175541563	Speak for Yourself by Richard Denny, PB, 2002	195.00
	817554158X	Succeed for Yourself by Richard Denny, PB, 2002	195.00
		THE SUNDAY TIMES CREATING SUCCESS SERIES	
	8175541245	Be Positive by Phil Clements, PB, 2000	140.00
	8175541253	Business Etiquette by David Robinson, PB, 2000	140.00
	8175541814	Communication at Work by Judith Taylor, PB, 2000	140.00
	8175541261	Develop Your Assertiveness by Sue Bishop, PB, 2002	140.00
	817554127X	Develop Your NLP Skills by Andrew Bradbury, PB, 2000	140.00
	8175541849	Developing Your Staff by Patrick Forsyth, PB, 2002	140.00
	8175541822	E-Business Essentials by Matt Haig, PB, 2002	140.00
	817554175X	Empowering People by Jane Smith, PB, 2002	140.00
	8175541733	How to Beat Your Competitors by John G Fisher, PB, 2002	140.00
	8175541342	How to Generate Great Ideas by Barrie Hawkins, PB, 2002	140.00
	8175541288	How to Manage Organisational Change by David E. Hussey, PB, 2000	140.00
	8175541369	How to Motivate People by Patrick Forsyth, PB, 2000	140.00
	8175541741	How to Run a Successful Conference by John G Fisher, PB, 2002	140.00
	8175541792	How to Write a Business Plan by Brian Finch, PB, 2002	140.00
	8175541296	How to Write a Marketing Plan by John Westood, PB, 2000	140.00
	8175541768	Improve Your Communication Skills by Alan Barker, PB, 2002	140.00
	8175541857	Improving Employee Performance by Nigel Harrison, PB, 2002140.00	
	817554130X	Make Every Minute Count by Marion E Haynes, PB, 2000	140.00
	8175541318	Make That Call! By Iain Maitland, PB, 2000	140.00
	8175541830	Making Innovation Happen by Michael Morgan, PB, 2002	140.00
	8175541326	Organise Yourself by John Caunt, PB, 2000	140.00
	8175541873	Performance Appraisals by Bob Havard, PB, 2002	140.00
	8175541865	Stay Confident by John Caunt, PB, 2002	140.00
	8175541334	Successful Presentation Skills by Andrew Bradbury, PB, 2002	140.00
	8175541881	Successful Project Management by Trevor Young, PB, 2002	140.00
	8175541776	Team Building by Robert B Maddux, PB, 2002	140.00
	8175541350	Write That Letter by Iain Maitland, PB, 2000	140.00
		TESTING	
	8175541660	Book of IQ Tests by Ken Russell PB, 2002	175.00
	8175541652	Career Aptitude & Selection Tests by Jim Barrett, PB, 2002	175.00
	8175541598	How to Master Personality Questionnaires by Mark Parkinson, PB, 2002	150.00
	8175541601	How to Mater Psychometric Tests by Mark Parkinson, PB, 2002	150.00
	817554161X	How to Pass Numeracy Tests by Harry Tolley & Ken Thomas, PB, 2002	150.00

QTY	ISBN	Title/Author/Binding/year	Price Rs.
	8175541628	How to Pass Verbal Reasoning Tests by Harry Tolley, PB, 2002	150.00
	8175541636	How to Succeed At An Assessment Centre by Harry Tolley , PB, 2002	150.00
	8175541377	Test Your IQ by Ken Russell, PB, 2000	195.00
	8175541644	Test Your Own Aptitude by Jim Barrett & Geoff Williams, PB, 2002	175.00
	8175541385	Test Yourself! By Jim Barrett, PB, 2000	195.00
		TRAINING	
	8175541210	Tales for Trainers by Margret Parkin, PB, 2000	195.00
	8175541202	Training on a Shoestring by Kaye Thorne, PB, 2002	175.00
		TRAINING ACTIVITIES SERIES	
	8176490172	Assertiveness Skills Training by Sue Bishop, PB, 1999	195.00
	8176490091	Counselling Skills Training by Philip Burnard, PB, 1999	195.00
	817649013X	Facilitating Learning by Tony Spinks, PB, 1998	195.00
	8176490180	Faultless Facilitation by Lois B Hart, PB, 1999	195.00
	8176490083	Icebreakers by Ken Jones, PB, 1999	195.00
	8176490075	Interpersonal Skills Training by Philip Burnard, PB, 1999	195.00
	8176490121	Leadership Training by Elizabeth Christopher, PB, 1999	195.00
	8176490164	Managing Recruitment Training & Development by E Christopher, PB, 1999	195.00
	8176490156	Outdoor Training by Bill Krouwel, PB, 1999	195.00
	8176490113	Role Plays by David Turner, PB, 1999	195.00
	8176490148	Team Building by Glenn M Parker, PB, 1999	195.00
	8176490105	Training for Change by Sue Bishop, PB, 1999	195.00
		GENERAL	
	8175541911	Bite-Size Sales Tips by Neil Watson & Steve Hurst, PB, 2002	145.00
	8175541237	Creating Customers by Pat Weymes, PB, 2000	450.00
	8175541415	E-Business Start-Up by Philip Treleaven, HB, 2001	695.00
	8175541199	Everything You Need to Know About Marketing by P Forsyth, PB, 2000	110.00
	8175541407	How to be an Even Better Manager by Michael Armstrong, PB, 2000	325.00
	8175541903	Plan to Win by Steve Smith, PB, 2002	145.00
	8175541091	Strategic Brand Management Creating and Sustaining Equity Long Term by J N Kapterer, PB, 2000	395.00
	8175541423	The First Time Manager by M J Morris, PB, 2000	195.00
	8175541547	2000 Tips for Teachers by Nick Packard PB, 2000	395.00

Distributors

VIVA BOOKS PRIVATE LIMITED

4262/3, Ansari Road, **New Delhi-110 002**
Tel. 3258325, 3279280, 3283121, 3285874, Fax. 0091 11 3267224,
e-mail: viva@mantraonline.com

214 New Apollo Industrial Estate, 2nd Floor, Mogra Lane, Andheri (E), **Mumbai-400 069**
Tel : 8235664, Fax : 8343383, e-mail : vivabooks@mantraonline.com

7 Aziz Mulk Seventh Street, Thousand Lights, **Chennai-600 006**
Tel : 8290304, 8294241, e-mail : vivachennai@mantraonline.com

6-A, Rifle Range Road, **Kolkata-700 019**
Tel : 2815431, 2816713 e-mail : vivakolkata@mantraonline.com

Foreword

Salespeople, let's face it, are the heroes in the workplace, the champions of the world of business.

Managers may well run the show, or at least create that illusion; finance and administration do most of the nuts-and-bolts stuff, do the most to make things work; marketeers jump through their hoops. All are worthy, yet salespeople walk the wire, the higher the better, and definitely without a net, and for them is reserved the glory.

These heroes, these salespeople, travelling up and down the land like latter-day white knights, follow a true path towards their target, their holy grail. These heroes, these salespeople, tough as you like, never doubt, learning, changing, moving ever onwards towards success.

The best can take the spills in their stride, springing stronger from the fall. The best know the truth – all may enter, yet there is room for only the few. The best win more than the rest, earn their place in the spotlight and then let their results do the talking.

And if, with your handy X-ray specs, you looked hard at the briefcase in the hero's hand, there you will see it, a special tome. Under the order pad, beside the gold pen, watch, money clip and medal, there you will see this well-thumbed, much used special book, *Bite-Size Sales Tips*, a book of advice for modern-day heroes.

You hero, you salesperson: go forth and sell, and take this book with you on the journey. Use it like an oracle, words of wisdom to send you forth with a focus – soundbites of good sense to make you shine.

You hero, you salesperson, this is your book.

Alisdair Chisholm
Managing Director of Marcus Bohn Associates
and publisher of The Achievement Report

'I need problems, a good problem always makes me come alive'
– Tiny Rowland

Introduction

This book of bite-size sales tips is the result of inspiration born out of frustration.

It is born out of the frustration of a hard-working sales professional who wanted to get practical, cost-effective sales training presented in a lively, informative, entertaining, yet thought-provoking way, understanding and empathizing with the hectic working lifestyle that goes with the territory.

It is born out of the frustration of a hard-working sales professional toiling away at the sharp end, dealing face-to-face with customers on a regular basis, and feeling there was precious little help out there, nobody who really understood.

It is born out of the frustration of a hard-working sales professional knowing exactly what he wanted, yet being unable to get it – anywhere.

This sales professional became convinced there must be many thousands of others in a similar position to himself, keen to get practical ideas and help on all aspects of the sales process, but not having a clue where to get it.

So this sales professional – one of the co-authors of this book – was inspired to do something about it. And this book of bite-size sales tips is the result.

The first thing he did was find somebody with publishing experience who could help him achieve his aims. He found the person through a local enterprise agency, and that person – you've guessed it – is the other co-author of this book.

The two teamed up and decided that the best initial vehicle for their bite-size sales tips would be a magazine – a working lifestyle magazine encompassing all aspects of one of the most important, and misunderstood, professions of them all.

This vehicle was *CoatHanger – The Sales Driver*, a magazine written by sales people for sales people. And if this book inspires you, then you would have also been inspired by the magazine.

They launched the magazine after six months solid research into the marketplace. They made sure every single issue was choc-a-bloc with bite-size sales tips. Word of mouth and anecdotal evidence quickly pointed to the bite-size sales tips being the jewel in the crown of the magazine, the ace in the pack, the unique selling point, the inspiration to sell more.

An in-depth reader survey confirmed the anecdotal evidence. More than 70 per cent of the salespeople who responded to the survey named the bite-size sales tips as their favourite section of the magazine. The one that provided them with the most value. The one that best helped them improve their sales performance. The one that truly inspired them.

There was no point in delaying the inevitable. Salespeople were crying out for it, and it would have been rude not to let them have it. Here it is, *Bite-Size Sales Tips*. An end to all that frustration and, fingers crossed, a new beginning for inspiration.

'The meek shall inherit the earth, but they'll never increase market share'

– William Gowan

1

Just starting out – basic selling tips

The buzz from getting the order can be better than sex

Selling can be one of the most rewarding professions of them all. The buzz that comes from clinching an order is one of the biggest thrills going – many who experience it say it is better than sex.

While this may say more about the quality of their sex lives than anything else, the sales buzz *is* highly addictive. That is why so many people make a successful and hugely rewarding lifetime career out of selling, and could not imagine doing anything else. Selling gets into their blood and they need that regular fix.

On the other side of the coin, selling can be one of the most frustrating, stressful and demoralizing ways of making a so-called living. This profession can burn people out in just a couple of years, or less, and do untold long-term damage to health.

That is why it is important for anybody embarking on a career in sales to make sure they get things right – right from the start. If you start off with bad habits then it is likely that you will never realize your true potential. You will get demoralized and probably end up doing something else.

In sales, first impressions are lasting impressions, people buy from people, your altitude is determined by your aptitude. These are just a few of the hundreds of sales clichés that litter the industry.

Clichés normally become clichés because they are based on fact. And this is very much the case in a business where personal contact is of paramount importance.

It is interesting to note that most sales leaders believe that face-to-face contact is set to become an even more important aspect of successful selling in the first decade of the 21st century. This is particularly illuminating bearing in mind that the continuing rapid advances in mobile communications technology mean that face-to-face contact is technically easily avoidable.

Selling revolves around building and maintaining relationships, and it is this basic truth that all salespeople must learn and remember so that it becomes second nature.

The best way to build and maintain a good relationship is by giving the customer what he wants, when he wants it, and at a fair price. You will note, therefore, that the twin themes of building relationships and keeping customers satisfied crop up throughout both this opening chapter on getting the basics of selling correctly, and indeed the rest of *Bite-Size Sales Tips*.

One of the newer sales 'clichés' is that salespeople are paid to be rejected. True enough. But the fact is they are paid a lot more when they are not rejected. If you get the basics of selling right then the frustration of a 'thanks but no thanks' will pale into insignificance against the 'better than sex' buzz of getting the order.

Oh no! Disaster story!

Finally, and after a lot of blood, sweat and tears (not necessarily in that order) I had managed to firm up the crucial appointment, the big one that would either clinch the deal, or screw it up. And this was no ordinary deal. It was for a contract worth £1.75 million, give or take a few tens of thousands.

Continued on page 21 …

'When a person tells you "I'll think it over and let you know" – you know'

– Olin Miller

Tip 1: be positive about the competition

Avoid making a negative comment about your competition. It is unprofessional and at the same time your customer sees a side to you that he shouldn't. If your customer has conducted business with the competitor in the past, you are not just criticizing the competitor, but the customer as well, and it could well backfire.

For all you know the buyer may be holding high stocks of unsold competitor's merchandise. By knocking the competitor all you will achieve will be to annoy or embarrass the customer further, promote confrontation and show that his previous decision was ill-judged. He will not appreciate having his nose rubbed further in it by you.

Non-specific positive comments about the competitor's product will offer empathy with the buyer. The customer will feel you're on his side and you then have an opportunity to emphasize your own company's (superior) products.

Tip 2: building blocks that lead to a sale

- Sell yourself first. Take an interest in your customers and they will take an interest in you. People buy people first, and products and services second. If your customers feel that you act and think like they do, they're more likely to warm to *you* as opposed to someone from a competitor who hasn't bothered to get on the same wavelength.
- Ask – don't tell. Asking questions keeps you in control. And asking questions helps you find out what customers want – and at what price they're prepared to pay.
- Sell results. Explain how your customers will benefit from your product or service. You're selling the result that it will give them – not the item. A customer buys something for what it does for them, so take time to discover what their *real* reason for buying is.

'It's attitude, not aptitude, that determines your altitude'

– All sales trainers

Tip 3: demand that training

Have you ever been in a situation where you've been dropped right into a selling job with only the very basics of training? Sadly, it's more than likely that you have. No training about the competition, nothing about the industry in general, and no in-depth study of the customer base – just a smidgen of product knowledge, a quick whizz round the office and a list of company car procedures. And get on with it, thank you very much.

That is not good enough. It's not good enough for you, your colleagues – or your customers.

Sales directors despair. 'Where do we get the time to conduct this thorough training – let alone the money?' they might ask. Although there never seems to be enough time to do things properly these days, people do manage to find time to put things right after they've gone wrong.

So don't be fobbed off if you're a trainee. And don't make false savings if you're a trainer. Whichever side of the fence you are from, good quality training is a must, and must be demanded.

Tip 4: don't moan about the customers – they pay the wages

Very occasionally we need to remind ourselves, and our colleagues, just who our customers are:

- They are VIPs, whether in person, by phone, by letter, or by e-mail.
- They are not depending on us to sell to them.
- They are not interruptions to our work, but the purpose of it.
- They are no match for arguments.
- They are not cold statistics, but instead flesh-and-blood humans.
- They are the most important people in our business. Without them we have no business.
- They are coming to us because they need something. It's up to us to provide it satisfactorily to them, and profitably to us.
- They are enabling us to pay ourselves our wages.

'Success is a great deodorant'

– Elizabeth Taylor

Tip 5: if you don't ask, you won't know

There's nothing wrong with asking a very open question to your customers about their future plans. Casually asking, 'What's new in the pipeline?' may give you lots of useful information about the company's projects, allowing you to be one step ahead of your competitors who don't think to ask.

If you catch the buyer in good humour he may well give you an insight into opportunities that are on the horizon. You may get the chance to offer products or services from your company never before used by that particular client. What's more, you're demonstrating a show of interest for the future of the company – a sign of commitment and willingness to help that no one can object to.

Tip 6: keep the customer satisfied – six golden rules

1. Treat everyone with respect and politeness, as you never know who may become a future customer (or boss).
2. Don't let emotions and feelings interfere with your attitude towards customers unless they are positives such as sincerity, concern and care.
3. Become the 'owner' of any complaint and don't let it go until you *know* it has been successfully dealt with. How will you know? Ask the customer.
4. Listen to customers – with your eyes! Watch their body language and don't just assume you know what they want, or what their problem might be.
5. Keep to deadlines, and reply when you say you will, even if it's to say you can't talk properly until the following day.
6. Don't say, 'Won't be a minute', because you will be, and it's better to overestimate, rather than underestimate, time delays.

'There is nothing more demoralizing than a small but adequate income'

– Edmund Wilson

Tip 7: new buyers – new opportunities

Don't groan when you discover there's a new buyer replacing the one you felt comfortable with. This is a fresh chance and a new challenge, not a hurdle to be dealt with reluctantly.

It usually takes new buyers around three months to settle into their new job. During that time he or she is on a steep learning curve about suppliers, products – and salespeople. Helping to ease the task now will reap rewards in the future:

- If you are an established supplier, remember that this is a golden opportunity for your competitors to break your hold.
- Use your first meeting to find out how new buyers think, make judgements and plan purchases. Find out about their past responsibilities and experiences. This will give you an insight into their capabilities and approach.
- Find out where the previous buyer is and, if still in the company, keep in contact. You never know when you might need an ally.
- When making your first presentation, assume the buyer knows nothing about you, your company or your products. Treat him or her as a new prospect. Take along as many brochures, price lists and samples as possible.

Tip 8: take rejection on the chin

Salespeople have to be thick-skinned to be able to do their jobs. They're being paid to be rejected on a regular basis. The key to survival and future success is to take the inevitable rejections on the chin and recognize the positives from what appear to be negatives. If you are not able to complete on a particular deal, you may still:

- arrange the next meeting;
- pick up any useful information about the customer, competition or market;
- get a referral;
- ask if you can be of help in the future;
- acknowledge any mistakes made, and improve upon them;
- leave a good impression of yourself behind.

You might not be getting a sale this time. But like a farmer, you will reap the benefits of what you sow next time.

'It's the difference that makes the difference'

– Jim Steele

Tip 9: how to deal with difficult customers

Mr Angry

Don't take the anger personally. Don't get ruffled yourself. Stay cool. Show empathy and don't look smug. Allow Mr Angry to finish, and let him expel all his hot air. Avoid telling him he's wrong, and try to move to a more private area if things really start getting heated. Don't say, 'It's not my fault' because that's no defence in Mr Angry's eyes. Tell Mr Angry what you propose to do, do it, and then check that all is OK as soon as you can.

Mr Regular Complainer

Listen, empathize and apologize, but recognize those who are simply trying it on – regularly. Compensation offered should only be appropriate for the size of problem. Be polite and firm, and avoid an 'I know you're trying it on' expression. Ignore what you might hear from colleagues about Mr RC, as these stories have probably become exaggerated over time. Remember that Mr RC is giving you regular opportunities to put things right and sell to him again.

Mr Quiet

Study him closely and watch for body language signs of displeasure. Mr Quiet will often say that everything's all right when in fact it isn't. Be extra perceptive and ask open questions about the level of service he has been receiving. Mr Quiet is the most difficult to deal with because you may only know that he's dissatisfied when the order fails to appear.

Tip 10: seven sales steps to Heaven

1. Make sure your objectives are quantifiable, measurable, and state *by when you want to achieve them*. It's no good just saying, 'I want to sell more widgets'. You need to say, 'I want to sell 35 per cent more widgets in the second quarter of this year, compared to the same quarter last year'.
2. Keep proposals *simple*. Don't tie things up in such a complicated way that the buyer's eyes rotate like the snake in *The Jungle Book*. Make things easy – and quick – for the customer to take in.
3. Know when to say *no*. You can't always be a 'yes man' (or woman). Sometimes your customer is only trying it on to see how strong you are. He will respect you more for standing up to him sometimes.
4. If your customer says 'yes' straight away, you've probably given away *too much*. But don't be too disheartened – at least the outcome has been positive. Just remember next time to negotiate a bit more from the outset.
5. Get organized and you'll be more *effective*. If you are organized with your physical effects such as your folders, notes, car and clothing, then your head will be organized as well.
6. Make meetings make things *happen*. There's no point simply discussing things that everyone already knows. Make action points, and define who will carry them out and by when.
7. Following up proposals shows your customers that you're *serious*. If you say you will call next Friday to find out the customer's reaction to a proposal, then make sure that you do just that. Otherwise it will be thought that you just can't be bothered. Not exactly the right message to convey, is it?

'Twenty per cent of any group of salespeople will always produce ninety per cent of sales'

– Robert Townsend

Tip 11: sit up and read the papers

Make reading the paper part of your morning work routine. No, we don't mean page three, or the TV guide, but we do mean the news, current affairs, sports and financial pages.

Look out for news snippets about your customers, and their customers, partners and suppliers. The more you know about the big picture, the more successful you will be in the smaller frame.

Keep abreast of current affairs. And keep an eye on sports news, even if you're not a fan. Having a basic knowledge of what's going on will help you with conversation openers, and prevent you from becoming isolated in a group situation.

Scan for details of personnel changes and staff promotions. And look out for the word on County Court judgements (CCJs) and receiverships relating to companies you may be doing business with.

Don't forget to sit up attentively when you're reading the papers at the office. Slouching back in your chair with your feet on the desk may just be giving out the wrong signals, however well intentioned you might be.

Tip 12: taking control of your time

Everything we do takes time, and we only have a finite amount of it – just like money. Prioritizing our activities for the day/week/month is just as much an important activity as the items we want to prioritize.

First priority: make a list of tasks, not in order of importance – just a list. Second priority: indicate a value for the tasks as 'A', 'B' or 'C':

- 'A' tasks are difficult, thought provoking, often new and unfamiliar – but important.
- 'B' tasks are easier, give quick results and often seem 'urgent' – but are less important.
- 'C' tasks are regular and trivial – and serve as excellent excuses for putting off the 'A' tasks.

Allocate 80 per cent of time to the 'A' tasks, and 20 per cent of time to the 'B' and 'C' tasks.

'Software cannot replace greyware'

– Anon

Tip 13: invite the boss out

Field salespersons talk every day to potential customers and get to hear what clients want and how much they're prepared to pay. They're the ones who are constantly juggling the balls between turnover targets, time constraints, stock availability, deliveries and head office backup – to mention but a few.

The boss is probably juggling the same balls although his (or hers) may just be a little bigger. The salesperson may be closer to the ground, while the boss may be closer to the whole picture. Both will benefit from a day out on the road together, as it gives the opportunity for common ground to be seen from two angles. Spending a day with a head office colleague is something to be welcomed, not feared, so don't wait around. Invite the boss out today.

Geof the exec

Geof wasn't bashful when it came to his achievements – but perhaps he was a little over boastful

2

Presenting your case – putting across the right message

Practice makes perfect when it comes to presentations

The art of presentation is one of the cornerstones of successful selling. You could have the best product in the world, and it could be just exactly what your prospective customer is looking for. But if you don't get your message across properly you could lose the sale and the customer will go elsewhere.

That way you both lose. You don't get the business and they end up buying an inferior product. Not good business.

The thing to always remember about presentations is that it is not just the product you are presenting. You are also presenting yourself. Both you and your product are in the shop window, and the customer has to be impressed with both for you to enjoy a high strike rate of success.

It is a truism that people buy from people, and they also buy into the benefits. They really do want to know what's in it for them. Buyers positively enjoy being presented to, especially when they like the presenter and what the presenter has to offer.

Some buyers, quite perversely, also get a kick out of putting a poor presentation into its place. Then, unless they are particularly twisted, they will do all they can to avoid being presented to again, certainly by the individual, and possibly by their company as well.

So, as with many areas of life, the first impressions made during the presentation are lasting ones. So it is important to get it right first time.

Many of the most successful people at getting a positive message across to the customer practise for hours beforehand. Sometimes this can be done, say, in front of the mirror, but often the most effective way is to rehearse in front of colleagues or friends.

Presentation practice makes perfect. Continual practice is often the best way to make a presentation look seamlessly natural. Rehearsal means results. Get the drift?

Of course there are some particularly gifted individuals who can go straight into a presentation, apparently completely unrehearsed, and make a fantastic job of it, such that the buyer is eating out of their hand. Well, the key word there is 'apparently', and those people are as thin on the ground as rocking horse wotsit, and if you happen to be one of them then it might be worth writing a book giving your own tips on how it can be done. You could end up a best seller.

In this chapter you should find enough practical tips and down to earth ideas that will help ensure you get positive results. Remember, there may be more than one way of skinning a cat, but buyers are a very different proposition.

Oh no! Disaster story!

Continued from page 5 …

The meeting was to be with the MD of a major company. I had already met with their marketing director and their IT director. I knew that I had negotiated my company onto a *very* short list of just two. The final decision lay with their MD, and the make-or-break presentation was going to be to him alongside his already-briefed IT director. On my side was our technical director. It was a bit like *High Noon*, but without the guns, cowboy boots, and that nice song that everybody thinks goes so well with the showdown scene in the film.

Continued on page 37 …

'Competition brings out the best in products and the worst in people'
– David Sarnoff

Tip 1: the AIDA approach

Every sales call is different, depending on the product or service offered, the benefits involved, and the customers' requirements at that particular time.

The AIDA principle can be applied to all calls, and adapted to fit the particular circumstances:

- **A**ttention: establish what's in it for the customer, and why he or she should listen to you. Show that you have bothered to do some homework about the client and industry. Suggest that you could be of help, with a general statement of potential benefits. Remember that products or services are not bought for what they are, but what they do for the customer specifically.
- **I**nterest: ask open questions in order to establish the customer's needs. Check that you are with the MAN (person with Money, Authority and Need). Remember to establish CFO (Criteria For Ordering).
- **D**esire: decide which of your products or services are relevant and relate the customer's needs to the benefits you can offer. Define the customer's objectives and how you can meet them.

Remember to convert FAB: Features to general Advantages to specific Benefits.

- **A**ction: know, focus on and ask for (in order of importance) specific actions you want the customer to make. For example, *sign the order*.

Remember to always have more than one plan or objective. Run through them before you make the call.

Tip 2: be humble and be honest – but don't waffle

In your sales discussion, don't be afraid to ask questions or ask for information and advice. Customers will see it as a sign of humility to which they may well warm. Nobody likes a know-it-all!

Don't ever make bold, sweeping statements, or assume things about your customer and his business. You may be dealing with several different trades and you can't possibly know all there is to know about each one of them. Every customer in every trade is different.

Be honest with all your answers to their questions. If you don't know the answer, admit it and offer to find out – it may be important to the customer. It may not necessarily win you an order, but it does go some way to getting the customer on your side.

And whatever you do, don't waffle.

'An ounce of image is worth a pound of performance'

– Dr Lawrence J Peter

Tip 3: did you hear the one about?

It's good if you're able to inject a presentation with a little humour, but be careful – some types of subject matter that may seem perfectly innocent to you can easily offend some people. Although you can afford to be less guarded when you know the person well, the best advice is to avoid potentially offensive material altogether, especially subjects like race, colour, politics, religion and illness. Even the paths of current affairs should be trodden lightly – you never know fully what the views are of the person you are talking to.

Of course there is nothing wrong with adding a light touch to the discussion, so why not poke fun at yourself? Then you can make others laugh with you at your own expense without any risk of causing offence. It also shows that you are thick-skinned and willing to take a bash, making your customer feel more comfortable in your presence.

Remember, you are still in a business environment, even if you're on different territory such as an exhibition or trade conference. Not only that, you never know who might overhear you and form a judgement of you based on an unappreciated sense of humour.

Tip 4: don't say

It is very natural to feel nervous and tense before making a presentation. It is a rare person who can just get up without any preparation and be able to spout out 20 minutes of meaningful dialogue. So don't torment yourself because you are not one of those gifted people. Instead, learn your subject matter, be prepared, practise first in front of a mirror and then in front of a friend – and remember a few golden rules:

- Never start off a sales meeting or presentation with an apology in the hope that your customers will indulge you with compassion. They won't.
- The listener's expectation will sink, and their attention will diminish.
- They may get cross if they feel their valuable time is being wasted.
- They will be waiting for your mistakes and slip ups, confirming to them your lack of competence you claimed at the outset.

So, even though you may genuinely be feeling awful, don't come out with things like, 'I'm feeling nervous' or, 'I don't feel well'. Keep your feelings to yourself and go and have a sleep in the car later. And definitely don't admit, 'I haven't had much time to prepare' or, 'I forgot some of the paperwork' or you really will be putting a spanner in the works – and winning no friends. Instead, smile openly, and try making eye contact with one single member of the audience – and imagine you are just having a one-to-one conversation with that person.

'A desk is a dangerous place from which to view the world'

– Anon

Tip 5: four parts to professionalism in sales

1. **Your own attitude**:
   If you feel like an amateur, you will come across like one. Act like a professional and others will see you in the same light.

2. **See people**:
   If you don't bother to make that last call, someone else will, and they will deserve to take your business away.

3. **Integrity**:
   If you stretch the truth, omit key information or avoid present difficulties, you may get the order today, but you will lose the customer tomorrow.

4. **Respect fellow salespeople**:
   If you are in a team that is strong, you will become strong yourself. Have respect for competitors' salespeople too, even if they do pinch your business. Find out why.

Tip 6: get to know about your company's advertising

It might well be someone else's responsibility to keep you informed about the advertising and promotional activities in which your company is engaged, but we all know that the quality of communication can be lacking sometimes, especially in larger organizations.

Make sure you get samples of any advertising, brochures and catalogues. Make it your business to find out how much things cost (sometimes customers accuse you of not spending enough on advertising). Bring good advertising to your customers' attention, and ask for their opinion (everyone becomes an expert, and everyone likes to be asked for their opinion).

Find out your company's future advertising plans and use the information to help your customers plan their purchases with you.

Make it *your* responsibility to find out what's going on. There's nothing more embarrassing than being told *by a customer* about an advertisement that your company has placed. You may well curse under your breath, 'Why wasn't I told?' but by then it's too late.

'Always be smarter than the people who hire you'

– Lena Horne

Tip 7: get the best from your written proposals

Easy-to-read proposals are the best ones to send, bearing in mind that the recipient is likely to be very busy.

Plan your proposal. Think first, then write down a brief outline before starting to write the proposal properly.

Be brief and punch hard. Get to the point without waffling. If you're not sure whether to include a certain piece of information, it's probably best to leave it out.

Don't cloud it. Use bullet points, avoid over-long confusing words and keep sentences short.

Sell it. Imagine you're talking 'person to person' and let your selling skills take over. In person you'd point out the advantages of your proposal from the customer's point of view, wouldn't you? Don't forget to include this in your written proposal.

Tip 8: make friends with your back-up team

It is very likely that for each and every one of your customers you are going to need some special help one day from someone back at the office. So it's important to make friends, not enemies, with all concerned – whether that's Brian in dispatch, Tina in accounts, Pauline in the sales office, or even Michael the MD. Who wins in the long run? Your customer, your company – and you.

Don't make a habit of 'bending the rules' too often, but learn how your company's system works inside out, so that when it really is necessary for you to pull some strings, you know exactly what your limits are – and those of your colleagues – and what the likely knock-on effects will be.

Remember to communicate with *everyone* who will be affected by the actions you take. Don't simply say, 'It's OK, I've cleared it with the boss' – that will just get people's backs up, and those people will be less willing to help you out next time. Get them on your side right at the beginning, and you'll be amazed at what you can get away with. Involve them and explain why you need special help.

'People want economy and will pay any price to get it'

– Lee Iacocca

Tip 9: proposals – 'dos' and 'don'ts'

Making and receiving a proposal is a fundamental part of the negotiation process. There are some basic 'dos' and 'don'ts' to consider – after you've decided who should open the discussion. Are you going to speak first, or are you going to respond? Your decision could affect the whole outcome.

Do:

- use humour only when appropriate;
- listen carefully to the other party;
- remember that buyers like to be sold to – so show you're making an effort;
- make conditional offers – such as, 'If you do that, we'll do this';
- use open questions – 'What if?' or 'How do you feel?'
- exchange information – don't just give it away;
- stall for time if you feel you need to – asking lots of questions may be one way;
- summarize the proposals at regular stages.

Don't:

- let emotions get in the way;
- start speaking until you've got something relevant to say;
- rely on memory to record points of detail – write them down;
- make too many concessions early on;
- make the customer look or feel foolish;
- ever say 'never';
- lose face by making an offer so extreme that you have to back down;
- answer questions with a direct 'yes' or 'no';
- forget to make direct eye contact;
- respond too quickly.

Tip 10: selling results

People don't buy things but they do buy what things do for them. The following are some simple examples.

A television set isn't bought for the box of electronics, it's bought for the entertainment that watching it will provide.

The farmer doesn't buy a cow at market simply because he likes animals, he buys one because it will provide milk that he can sell for profit.

People don't buy petrol to put it in their car, they buy petrol because they will then be able to complete their journey.

People buy results. Find out what results they want to achieve and look at what the product or service you are offering will do for them – not just what it is.

'The bigger the headquarters, the more decadent the company'

– James Goldsmith

Tip 11: speak the same language

It is easier to communicate effectively with a buyer if you 'speak the same language'. Listen to the way the customer talks and determine whether their speech is 'visual', 'auditory' or 'tactile'.

Visual examples

'I *see* what you mean.'
'I'll have a *look* at that.'
'Can you *visualize* it happening?'
'I can *imagine* that already.'

Auditory examples

'I *hear* what you're saying.'
'I'm all *ears.*'
'*Tell* me that again.'
'OK, I'm *listening* now.'

Tactile examples

'I *feel* OK with that.'
'Let's *touch* base soon.'
'I could really get to *grips* with that.'
'Yes, I'm *comfortable* with that.'

Then, once you have determined the language used, mirror it. This is particularly useful when talking on the phone where no body language can be used. With practice, it will be possible to mirror without too much thought, resulting in building up a subconscious empathy from the buyer.

Tip 12: softly softly catchee customer

The tone and volume of your voice accounts for around 40 per cent of the impact you make on others. So make sure it's well tuned, in order to ensure that more people will be happy and comfortable to listen to you – and can be more impressed with the content of what you are saying.

Be more aware of how others talk, whether they are conducting a meeting, talking to you one to one, or even if they are on the radio or television. See which people grab your attention for more than the first minute, and analyse what it is that they do to command your attention. You will more than likely become fatigued before too long if they are hollering at you rather than talking with you.

The same principles will apply when you are making a presentation to someone only a few feet away, as there's no need to shout to emphasize your sales points. In fact, you could try speaking more quietly than usual and you might find your customers actually becoming more attentive as they have to make slightly more effort to hear you.

Speaking more quietly can work particularly well when talking to a small group of people. Each person may be less inclined to interrupt as he or she may fear being branded a 'verbal bully' by the others.

'Selling has to be the most exciting thing you can do with your clothes on'

– John Fenton

Tip 13: write friendly letters

If you need to confirm appointments, agreements or quotations in writing, imagine how the letter sounds when read aloud. If it sounds like a friend talking it is more likely to be persuasive than if the tone is cold and abrupt – but don't be too informal as that will come across as unprofessional and unbusinesslike. And when it's in writing, it's permanent. So check and double-check for errors before signing and sending.

Geof the exec

Geof was glad he found a skip by the road – but perhaps he shouldn't have let his car get quite so bad

3

On the road – practical ideas on getting to your customer

You have to be well organized to maximize your sales potential

Selling is one of the most mobile of all professions. When you are in sales you often need to be where the customer wants you and when they want you to be there. Salespeople who turn up late for whatever reason are far less likely to get the order. And they may never see the prospective customer ever again.

So when you are out there at the sharp end, proper journey planning, appointment making and use of time are key factors in making sure you keep the wheels of commerce turning, both metaphorically and literally!

There is far more to being on the road, or on the tracks, or in the air than meets the eye. Being mobile means you have to be very well organized to maximize your sales potential.

Simple attention to detail, such as making sure you pack an overnight bag properly so that your clothes look pristine the next day, can make a vast difference to the impression you make to the customer.

Planning your route so that you can maximize the number of customers you see may sound obvious, but is often easier said than done.

And arrangements for meetings at minutes past or to the hour – say quarter past or quarter to – rather than on the hour will help to get you in front of more customers, because psychologically they will think less of their valuable time will be taken up.

Time is money. Yet another cliché used extensively in the jargon-packed sales arena but probably one of the truest of them all. If you can make the best use of your time when you are out there at the sharp end then you will be more successful. One of the sales tips in this section is '10 ways of getting an extra hour out of each day'. If we could all do that every day our income would only head in one direction, and it isn't south.

One of the most important meetings in any day is the last one. The temptation to cut the day short, especially when things have not been going too well, is sometimes impossible to resist. Yet often it is that last call, the one you really did not want to make, that bears the most fruit. Sod's sales law, that is.

Selling is – to some extent at least – a numbers game. The more people you put yourself and your products or services in front of, the more business you will do. And if you can organize your time efficiently, then your sales figures will reflect the fact.

If you arrive at a meeting calm, collected and coordinated then you will be sending all the right signals to the buyer. If you're all flustered, fraught and flummoxed because you are running late, or couldn't find the place, then you will be sending out all the wrong signals. That's no way to get the order.

Oh no! Disaster story!

Continued from page 21 …

Our team back at base had put a hell of a lot of work into this one, and myself and the technical director arrived at the meeting armed to the teeth with concrete responses to every possible question or objection their MD might raise. We had not, however, accounted for one thing… *my total stupidity.*

Continued on page 53 …

'Eighty per cent of success is showing up'

–Woody Allen

Tip 1: last call

It's mid-afternoon and your preceding calls haven't exactly produced the outcomes you had been hoping for. You think, 'Oh well, there's not much point seeing another customer now – it'll be a waste of time anyway, so I may as well go home and start again tomorrow'. Recognize this familiar scenario? Feel slightly guilty?

Making that last call of the day, instead of simply calling it a day, might well require that extra push from within yourself. But you've got nothing to lose and everything to gain.

Quite often it's the last call that produces the unexpectedly positive outcome, which would not have turned out that way if you'd left it for another time. On another day a completely new set of circumstances would have come to bear – not least the possibility that a competitor may have got in there first and spent all your customer's money.

And if your last call still doesn't give you the results you would have liked, you can drive home happy in the knowledge that you were right all along – but at least you now *know* instead of just *wonder*.

Tip 2: 'can I come and meet you at a quarter past? I know the way'

Arranging appointments is one of the key elements of selling. But getting that first meeting is not always easy, especially if your potential customer has already got a strong relationship with an existing supplier.

Don't ask for 'an appointment'. People make appointments to see their doctor or dentist and your buyer probably won't be all that keen for an 'appointment' to see you. To have a 'meeting' is far less threatening and a request for one will more likely be met with a favourable response.

Time is in short supply for busy buyers, so try asking for a meeting off the hour. By suggesting a quarter or half past the hour, the buyer will think that the meeting will finish on the hour, and will take up less of his valuable time than if it were to start on the hour.

Once you've got the green light, confirm the time, date and place of the meeting by saying that you've put the details in your diary, but don't spoil your success by then asking for directions. The buyer won't want to have his time wasted by explaining something that can be found out by other means.

When you've 'sold' your appointment, say that you've now put the agreed date and time in your diary and that you are looking forward to seeing him then.

'Every manager is a sales manager'

– John Ashcroft

Tip 3: 'dos' and 'don'ts' when you turn up 'on spec'

You turn up for a pre-arranged appointment with a potential new client in a town miles away from your base – only to find you've been blown out because they 'forgot you were coming'. What do you do? You decide to try your chances with another prospect in the area without an appointment.

Don't say: 'I was just passing so I thought I'd pop in.'

Don't say: 'My other appointment was cancelled so I thought I'd see you instead.'

Don't say: 'I couldn't find your phone number so I didn't ring first.'

Try saying: 'Instead of arranging a future appointment by phone, I wanted to take the trouble to make one in person.'

Try saying: 'I'm not calling to make a presentation *now*, I merely wanted to introduce myself in the hope of meeting you at a later date.'

Try saying: 'You're busy now, I know, but if there's any chance of me going off for a coffee and coming back a little later to see you, I'd be very grateful.'

By *politely* offering to fit in around the prospect's schedule, you have created a better chance of an appointment than if you had phoned for one – and your prospect may well be prepared to see you there and then.

Tip 4: taking out the boss

If you've been slogging away for ages to get a special new account, and you're nearly there but not quite, it might be time for a gentle prod in the right direction from the man or woman at the top. Your potential new client will be impressed that you're arranging for the most senior person from your company to visit them. And if you follow some simple rules of thumb your meeting should prove to be very successful, and form the basis of a long-standing relationship. (You may even get your first order out of it as well.)

- Prepare the meeting down to a T. Fully brief your MD about the customer, how much future business is possible and *the customer's potential profitability*. And tell him what you want his role to be in the meeting, and what you want to get out of it. His time will be valuable – so use it wisely.
- Plan the journey well – preferably together (so you can discuss things generally and informally).
- Lead the meeting at all times, making the introductions, and explaining why you think the meeting will be useful and what you think your customer will gain from it.
- Make sure that the two of you together don't come across as 'heavy handed'.
- Remember it's *your* customer. Let your MD introduce the background of his company, but ensure that *you* handle any specific negotiations.
- Don't interrupt either your customer or your MD.
- Remember to round up the meeting with a résumé of what action will be taken next, and by whom.
- After the meeting, offer to stop off at a pub, Little Chef or cafe, so you can have an informal chat about things. Ask for the MD's opinion and advice where appropriate (everyone has an opinion and everyone likes to be asked for advice).

'Monopoly is business at the end of its journey'

– Henry Lloyd

Tip 5: ten ways to get an extra hour out of every day

1. Get up at six instead of seven.
2. Make a detailed schedule and stick to it as much as possible.
3. Don't allow others to waste your time.
4. Tackle the toughest jobs first.
5. Combine tasks that are in the same area.
6. Keep a bag of envelopes, postcards and stamps with you in the car.
7. Call upon specialists to do jobs that you can't do yourself efficiently.
8. Work hardest in the period of the day in which you are most alert.
9. Tackle only one job at a time.
10. Go to bed at seven instead of six.

Tip 6: just why *are* you exhibiting?

Taking an exhibition stand at, say, the NEC or Olympia, is hugely expensive. Getting it wrong will cost dearly. Getting it right should pay dividends for now and the future.

One question to ask yourselves before you even consider taking part is *why*? Whether you are the boss, or one of the salespeople drafted in for the day, make sure everyone knows what they're doing there.

- Are you aiming to increase, maintain or recover market share?
- Are you probing a new market with a new product?
- Are you offering an existing product to a new market?
- Are you promoting a new product or service, or a new design or feature?
- Are you introducing a new brand, or showing off new technology?
- Are you there because your competitors are and you think you should be seen?
- Are you looking to get enquiries for you to follow up later?
- Are you selling on the day in order to maximize income?

Whatever your reasons for being there, be clear on your objectives and work out the ways to achieve them. For example, if your aim is to get enquiries, make sure to get some enquiry forms printed *before* the show starts. And then see that they *are* followed up after the show – and quickly.

'No one can make you feel inferior without your consent'

– Eleanor Roosevelt

Tip 7: cold calling to make an appointment

More calls = more appointments = more sales

A simple equation, but sometimes easier said than done, especially with the voice mail to contend with. You know the potential customer is probably there, but you have to get past the communication barrier first. The barrier was partly put there in order to fend off people like you.

Be prepared for the voice mail so that when your message is heard you come across efficiently and professionally. Simply leaving a message that asks for your call to be returned may not be enough. Try being specific about what the call is about, ie to arrange a meeting.

Use the IBROC technique.

- **I – Introduction** – introduce yourself and your company.
- **B – Benefit** – explain what's in it for them, briefly.
- **R – Relax** – relax them by 'not selling' to them over the phone (If you need to leave a message on the voice mail be sure to confirm your name, your return phone number and the time of your message.)

If you have managed to get through to the appropriate person, continue:

- **O – Option** – offer alternative times for an appointment.
- **C – Confirm** – confirm the appointment time, date and place ... and finish!

Tip 8: seeing customers who you think don't like you

If you are in a business that means you are calling on a regular number of customers, you will establish a number of contacts who naturally like you, and some who don't. Similarly, there will be some you like more than others.

If you have the freedom to determine your own monthly sales call cycle, it may be tempting to go and see your 'favourite' customers first. But it doesn't necessarily follow that your favourites are the most profitable.

OK, so you can have a chat and a joke, and you'll be sure of a cup of tea – but will the size of the potential order warrant the extra time spent there?

When you go to see a customer that you don't particularly warm to, or even one who you dislike, remember that there's nothing personal in it. You are making a business decision to make that particular call, based on the amount of anticipated trade that could come about. If it's just a cuppa you're after, we hear that Little Chef does a nice brew.

'If you do anything just for the money, you don't succeed'

– Barry Hearn

Tip 9: forget making courtesy calls without an objective

It's all very well making courtesy calls – so long as there's a point to them. Repeat calls on existing customers, or prospects, are a waste of time if all you're going to say is, 'Hello, how are you, nice weather today, is everything going OK? That's good. I'll see you again next month then'.

You may *think* that you are improving your rapport and relationship with the customer, but in fact courtesy calls are often detested by the recipient, because you are wasting their time. Remember – they are busy people too, and although they undoubtedly like you a lot, they don't want to stand around making idle chitchat.

So make sure you kick off with an *objective* to the call over and above rapport building. Think of *something* positive to discuss. A new product, a change within your company, a price change, or a special offer are some suitable examples. Or try simply asking some specific questions about your customer's business, products or customers. Everyone likes to talk about themselves and your customers will be no exception.

Tip 10: check out the presentation venue in advance

Gulp! You've just been asked by your sales director to make a presentation to 15 people at a venue that is unfamiliar to you. If it's at all possible, make every effort to visit the room in advance, so you can work out the optimum position to be situated for your 'performance'. It is essential to be seen easily by all delegates in order to gain *and keep* your audience's undivided attention. If necessary, arrange for a platform to be available. Pay particular attention to seating arrangements (enough for everyone), positioning of doors (for latecomers and 'natural breakers') and temperature (air conditioning can also be too loud, as well as too cold). If you're using visual aids, or relying on sound systems, then *make sure they work*.

Even if it's someone else who is actually responsible for setting up the room, you alone will be in the spotlight. So make it your responsibility to check out the room arrangements *thoroughly beforehand*.

'It's good to be out on the road, and going one knows not where'

– John Masefield

Tip 11: don't suffer from sales call reluctance (SCR)

It's quite normal to be reluctant to make those sales calls that you don't like making, so do yourself a favour and stop feeling guilty about it.

Here are 10 pointers to help you to recognize whether you are a sales call reluctance sufferer. If you answer yes to more than 50 per cent of the following statements, you could benefit from some corrective action that will help reduce those lost sales that you may be experiencing:

- I often feel that I am intruding on people when I prospect for new customers.
- I often hesitate when asking existing clients for a referral.
- I avoid giving presentations if I can.
- I tend to spend a lot of time shuffling my customer records around before actually visiting them.
- I sometimes feel uncomfortable about phoning someone who doesn't know me.
- I don't like initiating contact with new prospects for fear of rejection by them.
- I feel that making cold calls is difficult for me and makes me uncomfortable.
- I am relieved if I have to miss a call because of practical problems such as difficult car parking.
- I don't like promoting myself, which I feel is just not proper.
- I look for any excuse to delay seeing the customer who I'm sure doesn't like me.

Sales call reluctance can develop from a number of reasons when you are out there on the road. Simply recognizing that you sometimes suffer from SCR will help you to overcome it.

Tip 12: what sales directors do not want to see in their salespeople

Selling is the most important profession of them all. And don't you forget it. A sales director will go to increasing lengths to get the right people on his team because he knows that his company will stand or fall on the performance of its sales force.

So take a look at what the sales director does NOT want to see when you're out on the road. If you can see any of these attributes in yourself, quickly do something about it before it's too late. Because if the sales director sees it, so will the customer, and there is only one person who will ultimately suffer – and that's you.

Bad timekeeping: more and more emphasis is now being placed on high levels of professionalism in sales, and being on time for appointments and meetings (even if the customer does believe it's his right to keep you waiting) is an obvious manifestation.

Dodgy appearance: the way you look is more important than ever. Poor appearance and inappropriate dress sense are increasingly seen as definitely to be avoided in the competitive world. You don't need to resemble Brad Pitt or Liz Hurley to pass the dress test – just pay attention to the obvious: smart suits, well groomed hair and cut nails. Don't forget to clean those shoes – and leave the Marilyn Monroe tie hanging in the closet.

Know-alls: sales directors are always worried by employees who promise the earth. Experience tells them that those characters for whom no target is too high, and no problem actually a problem, invariably do not deliver the goods.

Achilles heel: to be successful in sales needs good all-round ability, including talent (there is often no substitute for a proven track record), resilience (you are being paid to be rejected, so roll with the punches), energy (especially important when prospecting for new business) and organization (self-discipline is vital to see the order through to completion, and ensuring customer satisfaction). Sales directors will frown upon identified weaknesses in any of these areas.

Geof the exec

Geof liked driving – but perhaps he should have realized that simply driving is not enough to succeed in sales

'Forgive your enemies – but never forget their names'

– John F Kennedy

4

Negotiation – the skill in selling

You may need to use the heavy artillery in the negotiation end game

Now we're getting down to the nitty gritty. Skilful negotiation is at the very core of successful selling and winning new business. More has been written about negotiation and negotiation theory than almost any other aspect of the sales process.

One key thing to remember about negotiation is that it is very much the end game in the chess match. If you are negotiating then you are within grasp of winning the business. This is the crucial time when holding your nerve will pay dividends.

So what is negotiation? You won't be surprised to know that the theorists and strategists have written hundreds of different definitions. All (well most) of them have some merit. Throwing our hat into the ring, we favour the view that negotiation is a process through which parties move from their initially divergent positions to a point where agreement may be reached. So there.

Ultimately, negotiation comes down to people and personal relationships between the negotiators. Yes, it is still, and always will be, a people business. Both sides will be striving to get the upper hand in negotiations. Buyers are trained in negotiation skills up to the very hilt. So the only way to stay in the end game is to match their skills with your own.

Key things to remember when negotiating are:

- What outcomes do you want?
- What persuasion methods are best?
- How are you going to manage the movement?

Through it all, never ever forget the value of being a good listener and the power of silence. If you can keep these ideas uppermost in your mind then it will help you deal with anything customers throw your way.

Buyers often use their heaviest pieces of ammunition in the end game. They use three main pieces of artillery, all designed to get the upper hand, and each needs to be neutralized in turn. The weapons in question spell FUD – one of the sales industry's many thousands of acronyms. **F**ear about the market. **U**ncertainty about the need. **D**oubt about the transaction. Once you understand the weapons in their armoury and how they are used, you will be prepared to turn them to your advantage. Send the FUD a Scud.

Of course, negotiation does not need to be a war, and if it does turn into full-scale conflict then you have a major problem. If, at the end of the end game, either party is not happy with the end result then the chances of a long-term relationship are pretty slim.

Both sides need to feel they have done a good job, otherwise the deal will eat away at whoever feels hard done by, and ultimately it will sour the relationship. To be a good negotiator you will always be looking for the other party to use their discretion in your favour. A truly good result is one that satisfies you and still leaves the other side happy to come back to do more business. And remember, always leave them the bus fare home!

Oh no! Disaster story!

Continued from page 37 …

The MD's office was large – very large. He sat rather nonchalantly at an old mahogany desk. There were several classy looking paintings on the wall, which I thought must be originals, judging by the expensive frames and individual lighting for each one. His secretary ushered us over to a coffee table in the corner of his office. The MD joined us and we engaged ourselves in the kind of conversation that people engage themselves in when they know they are about to talk about something far more important. This is where I made the *biggest ever mistake* in my otherwise illustrious sales career.

Continued on page 69 …

'If you see a bandwagon, it's too late'

– James Goldsmith

Tip 1: adapt to the situation

Every selling situation is unique to particular times, people involved and individual circumstances. Salespeople can sometimes be accused of inconsistencies, but *flexibility* is the key to meeting the challenges of different situations.

Consider those of your customers who place *some* of their business with one of your competitors. You offer four reasons to the client as to why you should get all their business:

- 'Your extra business would qualify you for higher volume discounts.'
- 'You would benefit from becoming a major account, enjoying priority service.'
- 'We could hold higher stock levels for your call off.'
- 'You would save money by maintaining only one purchase account instead of two.'

Now consider the prospective client who currently gives *all* their business to your competitor. You need to offer four reasons why the prospect should give you some of their business:

- 'It would give you an alternative source in case you are ever let down on supply.'
- 'Competition is healthy and reduces complacency.'
- 'It would give you an opportunity to compare the performance and efficiency of two suppliers so you can decide who is the better.'
- 'We would match the price being offered by the main supplier, so that you would not suffer any penalty for splitting the order.'

Is this being two-faced, or simply *adapting* and presenting a *positive proposition* for both scenarios?

Tip 2: assertive versus aggressive

There is a very fine line between assertion and aggression. Too far away from assertion becomes unsure, indecisive, and is just as much a turn off for the customer as aggression is.

Aggressive examples	*Assertive examples*
Sell	Help
'I...'	'We...' or 'It seems that...'
'But...'	'However...'
'Why?'	'For what reason?'
Eye contact stare	Eye contact showing interest
Finger pointing, table prodding	Open palms
Too much courage of conviction	Consideration of other person's viewpoints
'Do you want...?'	'What if we...?'
Interrupting mid-sentence	Waiting for a pause
'You are...'	'Are you...?'

'Growth is the goal, profit is the measure, security is the result'

– Owen Green

Tip 3: real objections, or just an excuse?

When selling to potential customers you will of course come up against objections. But are they genuine objections or simply excuses to get you off the customer's back? Don't forget to ask as many questions as possible to help you find out.

Your prospect may be raising objections that he thinks you cannot overcome. And that may well be the case, but you can try calling his bluff.

'OK, so if we did change the colour to yellow, did bring forward the delivery time by two days, did add a widget here and here and did reduce the price by £1, could I now have your order?' You haven't yet promised to do any of those things, and you actually may not be able to do so until you have investigated further. But you are at least establishing some idea of how your customer operates.

If he then goes on to raise further fresh objections, you start to get a pretty clear indication of where he's coming from. Although it is never easy to let go of potential business, in some instances, if you are sure you are being given a complete runaround, your time might be better spent concentrating on different prospects.

Tip 4: a sale is not a sale until it's ordered, delivered and paid for

Have you ever walked away from a meeting with a great order in your hand, but you felt there's something not quite right? Maybe the presentation went too smoothly, or closing the deal was just a tad too easy. You send off the order to your head office and move on to the next customer, but a couple of days later you get a call from your despatch department to say the consignment hadn't been accepted. Your early suspicions were right and your customer has had a change of heart (nice of them to let you know though).

Why did your customer do that? Possible reasons for 'buyer's remorse' could be:

- They felt they were over-pressured into ordering.
- They were later afraid that their decision may upset a colleague for some reason.
- They couldn't really afford the price.
- It wasn't really what they wanted in the first place.

You may be able to salvage something from the order by finding out what was wrong and changing it. But unless the customer is 100 per cent happy, you're still going to have trouble in getting paid to terms. And the sale doesn't really count until that time and until the money is in the bank.

'Facts do not cease to exist because they are ignored'

– Aldous Huxley

Tip 5: dealing with breakdowns in negotiations

If you can see that a breakdown is on the horizon, it is vital in most cases to prevent things becoming irretrievable. The longer things are left to fester the more inevitable it is that personal feelings will get in the way and nobody will win.

If someone from the party has actually walked out of a meeting in anger, try to get that person's colleagues to persuade him or her to come back. If their whole team leaves, apart from the fact that you really have got a problem on your hands, get your Good Guy (the one from your team who has the best relationship with them) to try to bring them back immediately.

Limit any damage by communicating as quickly as possible. A continued or, later, face-to-face meeting may be best but it may be more appropriate to make the right overtures for reconciliation in writing. Consider sending an e-mail, which is private and fast.

Before going to all the effort of healing the rift, consider if the consequences of no deal at all are worse for you than some deal. There will be some extreme instances when it's best to simply let things go.

Tip 6: no apologies here

Whether you are just entering the world of selling for the first time or you've been doing it for 20 years and think you know every trick in the book, there is one essential tip never to be forgotten, for which we make no apology for including here. A few times, just for luck. Think of it every time you are with your customer:

Don't be afraid to ask for the orderDon't be afraid to ask for the orderDon't be afraid to ask for the orderDon't be afraid to ask for the orderDon't be afraid to ask for the orderDon't be afraid to ask for the orderDon't be afraid to ask for the orderDon't be afraid to ask for the orderDon't be afraid to ask for the order.

Then say thanks and leave.

'I've got 32 jobs at the moment'

– John Harvey-Jones

Tip 7: selling ideas to the boss

Do you sometimes have a good idea that you think will have a positive effect at work, but then hesitate to put it forward? You might be fearful of being considered a troublemaker, or causing offence with your colleagues. Or worse still, of looking a fool.

So, overcome these fears by:

- preventing surprise that may give rise to opposition by discussing your idea with affected colleagues;
- preparing your facts and *selling* your idea to your boss. You are a salesperson after all, so your boss will *want* you to do a selling job on him (or her);
- preparing for a rejection at the first hurdle. It's natural for people to dislike change, and your boss is possibly no exception, so have a second attempt when the opportunity arises.

Modern managers recognize that a company's greatest asset may be its employees, along with their supply of fresh and practical ideas. If well thought through, your idea may well receive a better reception than you imagined.

Tip 8: use a PS wherever possible

When sending a sales letter to a client always remember to include a PS at the bottom. It is one of the first things that the recipient will look at, so get your strongest message into it, such as a special offer.

You can also try including two, or even three, PSs.

PS Use the first to name the number one benefit of your product or service.

PPS Use the second to restate the special offer – *with an action-by date.*

PPPS Use the third to state the FREE bonuses that are offered for ordering.

'The other man's word is opinion, yours is the truth and your boss's is law'

– Anon

Tip 9: the dangers of stereotyping

The selling world is becoming smaller. More and more sales drivers are dealing with customers from abroad, which gives a great opportunity to discover new and interesting things about other nationalities.

Some people tend to stereotype others because of basic beliefs and prejudices. This is dangerous and potentially damaging to prospective business, especially when nations and cultural backgrounds are concerned.

It is damaging because:

- It can lead to further prejudice and strained relationships.
- Subconscious barriers are erected which affect attitude.
- Stereotyping spreads quickly and becomes more and more distorted.
- People who stereotype don't give a chance to be proved wrong.

When we stereotype a nation and its people we are unfairly putting them into certain categories. We're also attaching labels that are subjective without taking into account individual differences.

People are dealing with people – not the whole country. Remove stereotyping from sales negotiations and business will be rewarded.

Tip 10: proof of the pudding is in the selling

Most buyers are naturally sceptical towards anyone selling as they know the salesperson has a vested interest in making that sale. If a good point is put across by the seller, the reaction may be 'You would say that, wouldn't you?' It's up to the salesperson to back up his or her claims with proof. So stating a benefit that's particularly appropriate to the customer will be better if it's also linked to a feature as a means of that proof.

For example, a sponge dessert salesperson who says, 'This pudding is delicious' would do better if he backs up his statement with, 'because it's made with a unique mix of ingredients – try a sample'. The customer feels reassured because he can actually see, smell and try the proof of the argument, and therefore won't think it's simply a salesperson's ploy to get a deal.

'A corporation cannot blush'

– Howard Walsh

Tip 11: selling versus order taking

A lady walks into a greengrocer's shop and asks the assistant for two pounds of carrots. How many pounds of carrots were sold? Answer: None.

A lady walks into a greengrocer's shop and asks the assistant for two pounds of carrots. 'We've also got some lovely Jersey potatoes in today – just right for a hotpot – and the carrots are on special offer,' said the assistant. 'OK, I'll have five pounds of carrots then... and five pounds of Jerseys as well,' said the lady. How much was sold? Answer: Five pounds of carrots and five pounds of potatoes.

Don't simply order take. Be on the look out for opportunities to sell *extra* on top of the requested order. It could make the difference between nearly making and definitely breaking your sales target.

Tip 12: silence

Silence is golden, sometimes. Try increasing the amount of silence in your sales discussion. A silence at the right moment implies certainty on your part and puts a bold line under what you have just said.

It takes practice, and it may have to be a conscious effort on your part to begin with. Some people become embarrassed by a silence in conversation but it can be worthwhile, providing it's used in the right way at the right time.

A silence can prompt uncertainty in the other person, and can also imply that you are non-committal. Although selling shouldn't be a fraught game of nerves, it can nevertheless be a good tactic to use a degree of silence occasionally. A natural breathing point in the right places is good for the other person, too. It gives him or her the impression that you are just as much a listener as a sales talker.

But don't fall into your own trap, though. If you feel uncomfortable by a silence after your own question, do not allow yourself to say something that dilutes what you've just said. Just wait for the other person to make the next move – unless he or she is a professionally trained buyer who has been taught to stay silent also. You may as well pack up and go home if that's the case.

'Would you ever buy a used car from me?'

– John De Lorean

Geof the exec

Geof was trying hard to mirror his customer – but perhaps he could have found a slightly more professional way to do it

5

Customers – how to give them what they want

Most salespeople have absolutely no idea why they lose their customers

This is the Holy Grail. If you can consistently satisfy the many, complex, and often fast-changing needs of the customer then you have a great present and an even greater future in sales.

The only way you can really satisfy those needs is by identifying what they are, and the best way to do that is through consistently high levels of communication. One of the current buzz phrases in sales is customer relationship management, or CRM – which, though quite a grand-sounding phrase, boils down to one thing – keeping a customer once you've got one.

The importance of retaining customers can not be overestimated. It costs a darn sight more to get a new customer than keep an existing one. And the old adage that the top 10 per cent of your customers will provide you with 90 per cent of your business is only an old adage because it is true.

One thing is for sure. Your customers will not be completely happy all of the time. Complaints go with the territory. Your ability to deal positively with dissatisfaction will be a cornerstone of your sales success – or otherwise.

And it is important to remember that a dissatisfied customer will not manifest that dissatisfaction by using anything so obvious as a letter or e-mail of complaint or an earbashing down the mobile phone. Most companies have absolutely no idea why they lose their customers. That bald fact is one of the most disturbing elements of the whole selling process.

It is not exactly rocket science to suggest that if we knew how to keep our customers satisfied then we would not be in the embarrassing position of losing them and not having a clue as to why.

If we can anticipate, and pre-empt, that dissatisfaction and do something positive about it then we truly have arrived as successful sales people for the 21st century. This is where the technology of CRM can help – by identifying the individual needs of customers. But computer printouts and projections are by no means the be all and end all.

Over two-thirds of customers switch suppliers because they are unhappy with staff service and attitude, whereas only 14 per cent move because of the actual product that is being delivered to them. It all comes back to the fact that sales is a people business. People buy from people and they won't buy if they are not getting the level of personal service they require.

One of the tips in this chapter looks at six golden rules to make sure you keep a customer once you have won his or her business. If you take on board these half-dozen basic rules, and apply them consistently, then you will reap the rewards that you will justly deserve.

Oh no! Disaster story!

Continued from page 53 …

On the coffee table was an antique-looking vase. It was apparent to me that the MD was either an art or antique collector – or possibly both (I have always been remarkably quick on the uptake). Keen to establish some common ground before we got down to the nitty gritty, I drew attention to the vase and asked the MD about its antecedents (you can always look that one up in the dictionary). I was surprised when he said he was not sure how old it was, or where it had come from. Anxious to build the rapport, I picked up the vase to inspect the markings on its base. Unfortunately for me the vase was full of water, at least it was until I picked it up to inspect the markings on its base. The water spilled out, dividing itself roughly equally between the MD's lap, the IT director's laptop, and our presentation folder.

Continued on page 85 …

'A friend in the market is better than money in the chest'

– Thomas Fuller

Tip 1: complaints

It should be recognized that complaints are opportunities to sell again and should go to the top of the action pile – not the bottom.

Establish trust with the customer by:

- Acknowledging their right to complain.
- Saying sorry, without justification.
- Being glad the complaint was brought to your attention.
- Offering options to the customer to rectify the situation.
- Asking which option would make the customer happy.
- Telling the customer what you are going to do about it – and do it.

In a survey of why customers switched suppliers, it was found that:

- 1 per cent died;
- 3 per cent moved away;
- 5 per cent simply looked around;
- 9 per cent specifically looked for better prices;
- 14 per cent were dissatisfied with the product;
- 68 per cent were dissatisfied with staff, service and attitude.

Sixty-eight per cent of all customers surveyed were dissatisfied because they thought they were taken for granted. Remember the Van Morrison song (also sung by Rod Stewart), *Have I Told You Lately That I Love You?*, and apply it to your regular customers.

Tip 2: customer objections

There are two main types of customer objections: excuses in order to avoid making or stating a decision, and genuine areas of concern.

A statement here is a positive sign of interest. Pre-empt an objection. This will show integrity and honesty. Then turn the objection into a positive by emphasizing what will be done to overcome it.

Listen – and welcome the objection. Remember that it is not a personal attack so don't go on the defensive. Pause before replying.

Don't fear objections, use the FEAR technique to overcome them:

- **F**ind the real reason. Ask for clarification.
- **E**mpathize. Make it clear that you appreciate the buyer's point of view.
- **A**nswer. Either *remove* the objection by showing it doesn't really apply in this case. Or *accept* the validity of the objection and then *outweigh* it with a stronger argument.
- **R**econcile. Settle, harmonize, show compatibility.

Then agree, and move forward, together.

'Success is a matter of luck – just ask any failure'

– Anon

Tip 3: the handshake

The way you shake hands is, in effect, your business card without words. It is one sure way of making a first and last impression. Don't make it a lasting impression for your customer to snigger at after you've gone.

A limp handshake will be equated with softness and ineffectiveness. But don't hurt the customer by squeezing, especially man to woman. It is not a trial of strength. Take care that your hands are clean, dry and not clammy. A handshake is best if it is equal, so grasp the customer's hand with the same pressure that he or she is using to hold your hand.

When offering your hand for a shake, turn it upwards towards the customer, so as to indicate openness and friendship. And if you're cold before a meeting, warm up your hand. In your pocket. Preferably.

Tip 4: smile with your mouth – and with your eyes

Relationships begin with the first 10 seconds, and a friendly smile radiates warmth that will help you to conduct business. If you don't smile, your customer will be wary and doubtful of you, so a little 'smile practice' might be just the ticket.

Park the car in a secluded spot and look into the rear view mirror. Practise showing those pearlies for at least five minutes, so that your smile looks genuine. If it looks like it's hurting, you're not there yet, so keep trying.

When you do get the 'natural' smile look, see what happens to your eyes. They glow and change shape with a body language that builds trust. (Would you trust someone who can't look you in the eyes? No? Neither will your customer.)

'If somebody screws you once, shame on them, if they screw you twice, shame on you'

– Steve Hurst

Tip 5: of course they are interested – so stay in touch

Question: why are your competitors' customers genuinely interested in you and your products? Answer: they are already buying variants of the products you are offering. The generic benefits of the products do not need to be proved to them.

There already has to be a need for the type of products you offer. Otherwise they would not be your competitor customers.

Even a satisfied customer of your competitor will be interested in new developments in your product area and should want to be informed about improvements coming into the market. A visit from you should at least be worth his attention.

So stay in touch, because even though the competitor's customer may not be in a position to buy while he is still satisfied with what he's getting, all things must eventually change. One day he'll have to restock or re-equip. Then that will be your chance to get your first order from them.

Tip 6: what customers want most

Knowing a customer's priorities is more important than your own. By providing the former, the latter will follow as a matter of course.

Imagine what you want from a salesperson when you are a customer. It's likely that your buyer's priorities are similar to your own, namely:

- receiving calls that were promised;
- knowing how to get in touch with sales and service personnel;
- communicating with the person who has the appropriate authority;
- knowing that your business is important to the salesperson and their company;
- being kept informed about all relevant issues, including costs and productivity;
- suppliers accepting responsibility for errors that are in fact theirs;
- receiving personal attention and being addressed politely;
- being given realistic and honest information about delivery or potential problems.

'A positive something is better than a negative nothing'

– Neil Watson

Tip 7: keep customers aware

Make sure that you get your name in front of your major customers every six weeks or so, no matter how Anything that creates awareness is worth the bother – whether it's a Christmas card, a press release, an advertisement or a sales call.

Even if you think that nothing has changed much in *your* company since your last contact, it's still worth making a call on the pretext of finding out what's been happening in *their* company.

Tip 8: 'KISS' the customer to improve sales

A sales presentation is ideally a conversation that seems to naturally take your customers through three steps:

- **Step 1:** *interest* them. The best way to get anyone to do anything is to make them want to do it. So get them interested.
- **Step 2:** *ABC* them. *Ask*, so you can find out what's wanted. *Bargain* by using 'if… then'. For example, 'If the price could come within your budget… then would you be happy to go ahead?' *Correspond* and prove what you claim by demonstrating, showing samples, writing or talking.
- **Step 3:** *finish up* with them.

If you can provide what is wanted, at an acceptable price, you're nearly home and dry. But remember to actually *ask* for the business – and then don't take any more of the customer's time.

The last thing the client will want is an overlong, drawn out meeting which wastes his time, so remember to 'KISS' the customer – Keep It Short and Simple.

'Creditors have better memories than debtors'

– James Howell

Tip 9: handing over a key account to a colleague

It happens to the best. You spend ages opening a new account and then nurturing it to become of major importance to your company – and your own sales figures – only to find that your company 'restructures' the geographical areas. Great! Now someone else is going to benefit from all *your* hard work. But don't be bitter; you're all batting on the same side (or at least you should be) and you must remember that the most important person in all the change is the customer.

The customer is *your company's* – not yours personally. Make sure you hand over customer details efficiently and effectively and check that all their expectations have been met, and that a proper introduction to their new contact has been made. Don't leave the customer high and dry – you never know when the next 'restructure' might occur, resulting in you getting the customer back again.

Now that you're out of it, remain available to give advice to your colleague if requested, but otherwise stay out of it and *don't interfere*.

Tip 10: what buyers want

Whatever selling techniques you've been taught on sales courses, you can be sure that experienced, professional buyers have been trained on how to counter them on purchasing courses they've attended.

Having the right personality, dressing appropriately and being professional are so fundamental to the job that they don't even warrant being listed. But the salesperson who can put himself in his customer's shoes and who can empathize with what the buyer wants is halfway there already:

- knowledge of their product or service;
- ability to keep promises;
- honesty;
- confidence of the support and backup from the salesperson's firm;
- willingness to help in a crisis;
- sensitivity to customers' difficulties;
- information and accuracy of information given;
- admittance of products' or services' weaknesses;
- sensitive response to price requirements;
- ability to see the overall picture of a situation.

'If you've got them by the balls, their hearts and minds will follow'

– Charles Colson

Tip 11: selling through intermediaries

Selling to the end user is one thing, but when you sell your product or service to someone who then sells it on to the end user, you need to use additional skills.

Once you have left your customer's premises, you have no control over how he is portraying your product to *his* customer, as is the case, for example, if you are selling to a retailer. The difficulty can be magnified further if you are selling to a wholesaler, who sells to a retailer, who then sells to the end consumer.

Aim to increase your customers' ability to convert enquiries into sales by *training their staff* about your product. In the case of a wholesaler, find out who their major customers are, and offer to train *their* staff. The business terms you offer might well be the best in the trade but unless the end sales staff are confident and enthusiastic about your product *and you*, your excellent terms might be irrelevant. Get yourself in front of the people who really have a powerful influence on what gets sold.

Remember: if it doesn't sell out, you can't sell in.

Tip 12: recognize your customer's style

When you deal with a customer on a regular basis, it should be possible to work out after a couple of visits just what type of character you're dealing with. It's useful to recognize your customer's style and tailor your approach accordingly.

You may know some of the following types already:

- *Mr Slicer* – You think you've agreed on a deal and he comes back for just a little bit more. Don't make it a deal-breaker, but be ready with an extra slice up your sleeve next time round.
- *Mr Toughman* – He likes to stomp around and bang the table with his hand. He shouts, 'It's not good enough.' Don't rise to the bait – simply respond in a calm, professional manner.
- *Mr Niceguy* – He's too sweet to be true. He offers to do things that don't come to fruition. Be equally pleasant but try to carry out all action points yourself. That way you know that they'll be done.
- *Mr Topoffer* – Don't give way to his request for your 'best offer' to be put on the table at the first hurdle. He'll only come back later to negotiate for more anyway.
- *Mr Heelsnapper* – Just like a terrier dog, he keeps snapping at heel and barking for more. If that's the way he likes to play only trade small concessions, and then only if you have to.
- *Mr Timid* – He just doesn't feel comfortable negotiating. Don't lose out on a deal because you go in too high expecting him to trade you down. He will prefer to have your realistic offer in the beginning.

'A desk is a wastebasket with drawers'

– Anon

Tip 13: make your sales letters spell out the benefits

When sending out a letter to attract potential customers of your product or service, put yourself in the recipient's position and imagine receiving that letter. Then imagine you know absolutely nothing about the product or service you are being offered. What is it that would turn *you* on?

Work out a 'what's in it for me?' list, based on your own extensive knowledge of what you are offering. Don't just think of the *features* but concentrate on what the *benefits* are to the customer.

Is your customer the end user or an intermediary? The benefits that he is looking for could be completely different depending on his role.

Make your letter short, sharp and to the point. Don't embellish the letter just for the sake of it. Then see if it passes the 'so what?' test. If, in your imaginary position of just having received the letter, you ask 'so what?' about the stated benefits, go back and think again.

Geof the exec

Geof had been told that he should make himself unforgettable – but perhaps he was going a little too far with his dress sense

6

Technology and communication – maximize their effectiveness

Mastering sales technology is better than a poke in the eye with a biro

The opportunities presented by the rapid advances in sales communication technology are seemingly endless. The trick here is to evaluate those opportunities and harness the ones that can offer practical help in increasing sales performance. Those that don't can – and should – be discarded

Take the Internet as an example. Computers can now talk to each other and share information. The advent of WAP (wireless application protocol) technology meant that the information available through the Internet became truly mobile.

Yet WAP was, and is, itself a largely text-based interim technology with severe limitations. With the all singing, all dancing 'third-generation' mobiles fully up and running there will, say the pundits, be more mobile dot.com activity than through fixed computers. Not only will fantastically sophisticated customer information be available but it will be available instantly wherever you may be. We'll all be living with our pocket Internet terminals.

All well and good. But it's not so much what you've got when it comes to using sales technology – more what you actually do with it that will matter. Take the humble biro. You can produce a fantastic sales proposal with it if you know what you are doing. If you don't know then you can end up giving yourself a poke in the eye.

The same applies to all forms of sales technology, from corporate software control packages applying to customer relationship management and sales force automation to tools designed specifically for the individual use of salespeople at the sharp end. And who knows what else is on the horizon? It can either work wonderfully for you or backfire badly against you.

The bottom line is that, properly applied, the Internet and all that goes with it can provide viable tools for salespeople. For a start, it is full of potential customers to whom you would find it very difficult to get access through, let's say, more traditional channels, such as the telephone. There is something of the novelty value here for prospective customers. In the same way that fax communications used to elicit an excited response in the early years, the relative novelty of e-communications remains. What's more, e-mails are still less likely to be screened than telephone calls. You don't have to worry about the gatekeeper preventing you from even talking to your prospective customer or letting him or her see your letters and/or faxes.

And yet the humble telephone, be it landline, mobile or video, remains the most important single tool of sales communication technology on the block, and shows no sign of not being so.

Developments in WAP-enabled 'push technology' mean you are able to provide unsuspecting potential customers, as well as existing customers, with a plethora of information in which, you have it on good authority, they will be interested.

Whether you love 21st-century technology and are willing to embrace everything that comes with it, or whether you hanker after the days of handwritten call reports and acetate OHP presentations, the fact remains that salespeople ignore the opportunities provided by technology at their peril. Use the good bits to your advantage and throw the bad bits into the online wastebasket.

Oh no! Disaster story!

Continued from page 69 …

Suddenly time began to go very slowly. It was a bit like in one of those Sam Peckinpah movies, where all the blood comes out in slow motion, or in that Clint Eastwood spaghetti western when the horrible bloke keeps getting his watch out and it plays that sad tune. The look of absolute horror on my technical director's face was matched only by the look of incandescent rage on that of their MD.

Continued on page 103 …

'When money is at stake, never be the first to mention sums'

– Sheik Ahmed Yamani

Tip 1: yes, that last call of the day *is* important

The day of the computer is here. Phones, faxes, e-mails, videoconferencing and other electronic paraphernalia are all well and good, but you can't beat meeting a customer face to face.

So when it is cold and wet outside, and the time is 4.30 in the afternoon, it is very tempting to head back home. But remember – within some markets 50 per cent of the selling effort is simply making the personal call in the first place. One extra call each day equates to around 20 a month, some of which are bound to turn into orders. If you make one less call each day, your sales turnover is only going to go in one direction – guess which.

Tip 2: getting the best out of e-mail and the Internet

The use of e-mail is growing fast. It is quick, versatile and user friendly – and it saves paper. You can also look at Web sites of other companies for information on competitors and use search engines for general research. Whatever subject you are interested in, it's almost certain that you'll find something about it on the World Wide Web.

Follow some simple rules to help get the most out of using the Internet for sending e-mails:

- Do control the quantity of communications – ask yourself whether you really do need to send the message. If not, don't.
- Keep messages brief – the shorter they are the faster they can be dealt with by the recipient.
- Don't put off your responses – it is better and more efficient to answer e-mail immediately and keep your e-desk clear.
- Bear in mind 'netiquette' – use meaningful subject titles, keep business and personal issues separate, never use inappropriate or insulting language.

Remember – the World Wide Web *is* the future of communications. Don't get left behind.

'The only place where success comes before work is in the dictionary'
– Vidal Sassoon

Tip 3: making records

Always take notes of deals and agreements you are working on, preferably during the meeting. If that's not possible for some reason, record the details immediately after the meeting while they're still fresh in your mind. Even though you think they may be fresh now, how fresh will they be after you've done another 10 sales calls?

Summarize your agreement in writing and send a copy to the other party. Make sure you include who gets what, what action points are needed, and details on how, by when and by whom.

Send the minutes straight away, so that any confusion or disagreement can be resolved quickly. Don't rely on your memory – this could be just the excuse you're looking for to get that laptop, electronic organizer or dictating memo machine.

Failing that, a piece of paper like they used in the old days will still do.

Tip 4: build up a portfolio of your clients

Whether you use old-fashioned paper and folders or whether you have moved into the electronic age with palmtops and notebooks, it is so important to keep a file on your customers – and your potential customers. Over time you build up a profile of them, their interests and past business patterns that will not only benefit you but will benefit your successor when you move on to higher heights. Your customers' folders should show a potted history of business activity – just like the ones you would have liked to have been handed when you took over the area.

Keep a pocket camera with you so you can also take a snap of your clients for your file – and for your backup office team. If you explain to your customer what it is for, they will be very unlikely to object. The people on the sales desk back at base will find it helpful to 'put a face to the name' and will find it helpful the next time they have to speak to the customer or do some paperwork about them.

Although it may not immediately result in an increase in sales, you never know what might happen over time. Anything that builds rapport between your customers and your company has to be a good thing, and it's the difference that makes the difference.

'If you can actually count your money then you are not a really rich man'

– John Paul Getty

Tip 5: lend audioconferencing an ear (and keep an eye on video)

Life on the road can be tough at the best of times: hours of boring motorway driving, heavy lorries, speed traps, contraflows, roadworks, and on top of all that, hastily convened 'emergency' sales meetings, often meaning an extra overnight stay.

Yet the technology is there to ease the extra burden caused by impromptu sales meetings. Audio/Videoconferencing is a viable, cost-effective alternative and is especially useful when the sales team needs to be pulled together at short notice, such as for a new marketing campaign or an unexpected move from a competitor. Here's an at-a-glance guide:

- Audioconferencing connects three or more people in a single telephone call. Set up is straightforward. Just make a single call to a teleconferencing supplier providing names and addresses of participants.
- Set up can be within five minutes of the original call, and will be handled by an experienced conference coordinator.
- No special equipment is required. Sales team members only need a telephone (or video phone).
- A small group of people sitting at a table could take part, or it can be adapted to the needs of hundreds.

Tip 6: time to ditch that diary and throw away that pen

You could argue that there is nothing wrong with a diary and a good old-fashioned contacts book. There again, you could also argue that the world is flat. When it comes to being efficient, especially when you are mobile, the days of paper-based technology are well and truly numbered. The new kid on the block is the hand-held personal computer (HPC) and it has already taken the place of pen and paper in many a mobile office. Here are some of the features of HPCs, and the benefits that they can provide for you:

- They are flexible and accurate, so you can adapt them to suit your own requirements, and you can be confident that they are not going to get things wrong.
- They are backupable, so you can be reassured that the valuable information will not get lost forever if you've also saved it on your office or home PC, unlike that old-fashioned filofax that you left in the phone box.
- The information they gather can be searched and shared, so you can save valuable time otherwise spent looking in all the wrong places and queuing at the photocopier – unlike your competitors who still can't find what they're looking for.
- They are downloadable, so you can send information to colleagues and customers at the touch of a button, quickly, efficiently and cheaply – unlike in the days when you packaged up a ream of paper and queued up at the post office, only for it to get lost.
- They are the future, so that you will not be left behind in the dark ages, unlike others who haven't yet woken up to what's going on around them.

'You've gotta keep the customer satisfied'

– Paul Simon and Art Garfunkel

Tip 7: don't let technology make a monkey out of you

Sales technology is a fact of life, and switched on salespeople will always be ready to embrace technology that helps make their job easier, and improves customer service.

But a word of warning here. Don't use any new sales technology until you have a pretty good understanding of how it works.

The sales professional who knows exactly how to use the technology at his disposal is indeed in charge of a powerful selling aid. The sales professional who goes out to impress a buyer with the latest gizmo and finds out he can't even switch it on will fall flat on his face.

The psychology of customers here is interesting. People are always willing to be impressed by professionalism so long as it is just that – professional. But if the professional doesn't get it right, especially where technology is concerned, then they can expect a high level of disdain to come their way.

So before you use technology at the sharp end, become acquainted with it and don't let it make a monkey out of you.

Tip 8: how to avoid the worst telephone mistake you can make

The most common and serious mistake salespeople make on the telephone is making opening statements that build resistance.

Within the first 15 seconds of a call you create one of two emotions within the person you're speaking to: resistance or interest. Nothing else.

Unfortunately most callers create resistance. The result is what they perceive as a morale-killing rejection alongside an early exit from the phone call.

They start with an uninspiring line like, 'We sell… and I'd like to talk to you about them.' The listener then justifiably thinks, 'So what why should I listen?' Here's another resistance builder to avoid at all costs: 'I sent you a letter and I was wondering if you received it yet?'

So what if they did? What are they supposed to say? 'Oh yes! Glad you called. I was just sitting here thinking that I should buy from you!' No chance.

Here's a simple three-step guide to success:

- Introduce yourself and your organization.
- State an interest-stimulating, curiosity-creating benefit that appeals to their desire to gain, or avoid loss. Failure to do this will mean no sale.
- Get them involved in a conversation. Remember, you want to do more listening than talking. Tell them that in order to deliver the potential benefit you alluded to, you need to get information.

'One man's wage is another man's price rise'

– Harold Wilson

Tip 9: join the industrial revolution of the 21st century

The Internet is to life today what the steam engine was to the industrial revolution of the 19th century. The Internet will change life completely and salespeople will be among those leading this new revolution.

If you want to be part of the new age then here's a few tips:

- Keep abreast of the rapid advances in mobile communication technology.
- Consider getting your own Web site – or at least your own page on the company site.
- Use the Internet as a provider of customer information. Many companies provide name and e-mail details of key personnel but *not* telephone numbers.
- Remember the power of sending an e-mail and that they are rarely screened. No gatekeeper to worry about.
- Be aware of the growing importance of voice recognition technology.
- Don't be put off by the bad press surrounding e-commerce – it will work for the right products and services.

The Internet will create an underclass of people who ignore technology – and it will be at their peril.

Tip 10: three key telephone tips

1. Set the stage. Be up front about why you've made the call and what your main point is. That way you'll engage the interest of listeners and help them to understand what follows.
2. Accept responsibility for them understanding. Blaming the other person for not understanding you is pointless. You cannot be responsible for their efforts – but you can be for your own.
3. Say all that's on your mind. Once the conversation is over, it's too late to say things that you left out.

'If all economists were laid end to end they would not reach a conclusion'

– George Bernard Shaw

Tip 11: technical jargon – if in doubt, leave it out

When selling anything slightly technical it is easy to slip into the use of jargon. That may be fine as long as you are 200 per cent certain that your customer knows fully what you mean. But if you are only 99 per cent sure, then it's best to only use terms and phrases that everyone in the conversation can understand.

Technical jargon ensures that only others closely involved with you or your industry can comprehend you – and forces others to switch off. If there are other people present who are less word wise you also run the risk of coming across as being downright rude to them.

Technical jargon users are members of their own exclusive club, so if you *have to* use your own jargon, limit it to when dealing with colleagues and peers – not customers. Customers may not understand what the heck you're talking about and may be embarrassed to say so. Limit the use of your customer's jargon to when you're totally confident of knowing what *you* are actually talking about as incorrect use will alienate you further. So, if in doubt leave it out.

Tip 12: phone selling

When making or receiving a sales call you don't have the advantage of having eye contact or body language so your positive attitude has to be conveyed by sound alone.

A checklist for telephone selling:

- If you receive an incoming call while driving, offer to call back when you have pulled over and have got all relevant information to hand.
- Check back over the records and keep notes about the call. Use a book or diary and not scraps of paper that fly out of the window.
- Find out the customer's requirements by using open-ended questions.
- Meet price objections with 'value' answers.
- Give the price with added information, for example, 'That includes delivery'.
- Stress the benefits.
- Explore other sales possibilities with the customer.
- If you don't have what is being requested, offer an alternative.

When selling on the phone (possibly from the car) it is essential to sound positive about taking the order and to gently nudge the customer into a decision to buy. Try being assumptive without being pushy and overcome potential objections by offering alternative options.

'A verbal contract isn't worth the paper it's written on'

– Samuel Goldwyn

Tip 13: follow the sales office rules – and make life easier for all

When you proudly send in a wadge of order forms at the end of the month to (hopefully) get you over target, spare a thought for the girls and boys in the back room who have to process them accurately and at the speed of light. Remember your induction session when you joined the company and you were shown what goes on behind the scenes and how it all happens.

Now's the time to make life easier for everyone – and follow those sales office rules.

Whatever technology is used at head office, make sure you cooperate with others, and you will find that your colleagues will bend over backwards to help you. So if the sales office requires an order form in triplicate, deliver it in triplicate. If they want an e-mail followed by a fax, give them what they want. It will help them to process your orders more efficiently, and therefore your customers will be pleased with your company's performance. Everybody wins.

That's not to say that the use of improved technology can't be added to the order processing system to create better efficiency. But having a go at the person behind the sales desk about things that don't run smoothly won't help. Wait until you can bring things up at the next sales meeting and then come out with a well-structured creative criticism – with suggestions for how improvements can be implemented.

Geof the exec

Geof thought that his new 'entire office in a case' was enough alone to win business – but perhaps he was forgetting that his customers still wanted personal service

7

Money matters – getting it all figured out

A mastery of figures and finances will add up to more sales

Any sale involves a financial transaction of some kind, and it is vitally important to know exactly what you are doing in the figures department. There's no point clinching an order if it doesn't translate into profit. You certainly won't get thanked for it and it could do untold damage to your reputation as a sales professional.

Most successful sales people are highly numerate. They may not have a natural gift for dealing with the financial aspects of the sale but they will make sure they acquire the skills necessary to stay one step ahead of the game when it comes to agreeing a price.

The more numerate you become the more financially aware you will be, and this will help you in both day-to-day financial dealings and in looking at the bigger picture in terms of you and/or your company's performance.

In this section of the book we concentrate on the practical side involved in your regular dealings with customers. A mastery of this area should do nothing but enhance your appreciation of the sales process *and* your appreciation of the paramount importance of the bottom line.

Every mobile sales professional should 'count' a calculator as an essential part of his or her sales tool kit. But there's no point having a fancy-looking calculator if you don't know how to get the best from it. Mastering the functions of a calculator, preferably a smart-looking one that is good for the image as well as practical, is one of the most important skills that the serious sales professional will learn.

If buyers sees a salespeople fumbling around with the functions of their calculators then it will do nothing to inspire their confidence. It might encourage them to feel that they have a psychological edge, and work harder at driving a better bargain for themselves. Worse still, they might not want to deal with somebody who doesn't know what they are doing. On the other hand a slick, confident approach that provides the customer with meaningful information quickly will have quite the opposite effect.

Cool use of the calculator will help you deal quickly with a whole roster of sales situations, from taking out the VAT, to comparing margins with mark-ups, to working out how much a price change will affect gross profit. And they come in quite handy as well for one of your most important financial transactions of any month... working out your expenses.

Get the figures figured out and you will figure in the future.

Oh no! Disaster story!

Continued from page 85 ...

I pride myself on my ability to turn negatives into positives. But when the IT director picked up his laptop and turned it upside down to let the water out over the coffee table it began to dawn on me that this was not the time. I found myself mumbling incoherently about paying for any damage to the laptop and any cleaning for the suit, when the MD said 'I think it best we adjourn the meeting to another time'. There never was another time, and I never did find out how old that vase was and where it came from. But I bet it wasn't worth the £1.75 million that went down the drain that day.

Continued on page 121 ...

'A wool seller knows a wool buyer'

– Thomas Fuller

Tip 1: taking out the VAT

For anyone who is too shy to ask, working out a price with or without VAT can be confusing. The calculations are simple if you know how, and you will no longer need to fidget with embarrassment on your customer's chair when he or she asks you what the net, gross or VAT elements are.

Assume VAT is at 17.5 per cent (but don't worry if rates change because the calculation principles are the same).

If you start with a price that you want to *add* VAT to, *multiply* by 1.175. (If VAT was at, say, 19.25%, then multiply by 1.1925).

For example, to calculate £31.72 plus VAT @ 17.5% then £31.72 × 1.175 = £37.27. The gross price, including VAT, is £37.27.

If you start with a price that *includes* VAT and you want to know what the net price is (ie, the price excluding VAT), then *divide* the original price by 1.175. For example, to calculate the net price if the total price (including VAT) is £37.27 then divide £37.27 by 1.175 = £31.72. The net price, excluding VAT, is £31.72.

If you start with a price that *includes* VAT and you want to know how much the VAT element is, then use the memory function on your calculator. For example:

- **Step 1:** £37.27 inc VAT. Enter £37.27 into 'M+' button. (It shows '37.27 M' in the display.)
- **Step 2:** divide by 1.175 and enter into the 'M–' button. (It shows '31.719148M' in display.)
- **Step 3:** press the 'memory recall' button. (It shows 5.550852 in the display.)
- **Step 4:** Round this figure down to £5.55: £5.55 is the amount of VAT included.

Tip 2: to fly or not to fly

For long journeys, it may work out to be more cost effective to travel by rail or plane, and hire a car at the destination, thus reducing the number of nights stayed away and cutting down on your valuable time. Not only can it work out cheaper but you also gain time to prepare your sales presentation and arrive more relaxed than if you had driven all the way.

Take, for example, the London sales manager who has to make an important presentation in Edinburgh. When in Edinburgh, it would be a good idea to make some prospect calls while in the area. Consider the options:

Option 1 – drive all the way

Day 1: set off in the morning, drive 373 miles all day

Petrol	£41.50
Midday snack	£5.00
Evening meal	£15.00
Lodge accommodation	£45.00

Day 2: Presentation at 10 am, followed by prospecting

Petrol to drive locally 100 miles	£11.00
Midday snack	£5.00
Evening meal	£15.00
Lodge accommodation	£45.00

Day 3: set off am, drive 373 miles all day

Petrol	£41.50
Midday snack	£5.00

Total cost: 3 days and £229.00
Side effect: factor 10 driving stress

Option 2 – fly/drive

Day 1: Set off in the morning, leaving car at the airport

Petrol to drive 20 miles to airport	£2.50
Flight on budget airline	£40.00
Evening meal	£15.00
24-hour car hire	£40.00
Lodge accommodation	£45.00

Day 2: presentation at 10 am, followed by prospecting

Petrol to drive locally 100 miles	£11.00
Midday snack	£5.00
Return flight	£40.00
Airport car park	£7.00
Petrol to drive 20 miles from airport	£2.50

Total cost: two days and £208.00
Side effect: factor 10 calm nerves

'The best investments are often those that looked dead wrong when they were made'

– Anon

Tip 3: you say mark-up, I say margin

The terms 'mark-up' and 'margin' are often confused and it is very important to ascertain whether the terms are being used correctly and that both parties are talking the same language, otherwise the end results can be wide apart.

There is a direct link between 'mark-up' (reckoned on the cost price) and 'margin' (reckoned on the selling price):

- a half of mark-up = a third of margin;
- a third of mark-up = a quarter of margin;
- a quarter of mark-up = a fifth of margin;
- a fifth of mark-up = a sixth of margin.

And so on, indefinitely.

To calculate what a 23 per cent mark-up would be on something that costs £20.00, then multiply £20.00 by 1.23, ie £20.00 multiplied by 1.23 is £24.60. (If you were calculating, say, a 46 per cent mark-up, you would multiply by 1.46.)

To calculate what a 23 per cent margin would be on something that costs £20.00, then divide £20.00 by 0.77 ('0.77' is arrived at by taking 23 away from 100; if you were calculating, say, 19 per cent then you would take 19 away from 100, and arrive at '0.81' as the factor). So £20.00 divided by 0.77 is £25.97.

To calculate what the cost price would be, if the market retail price is £25.97 and you want to make 23 per cent margin, then multiply £25.97 by 0.77 (Like before, '0.77' is arrived at by taking 23 away from 100).

ie £25.97 × 0.77 = £20.00.

To calculate what the cost price would be, if the market retail price is £24.60 and your customer wants to make 23 per cent mark-up, then divide £24.60 by 1.23, so £24.60 divided by 1.23 is £20.00. (If you were calculating, say, 34 per cent mark-up, then divide by 1.34.)

Practice makes perfect. Play around with your calculator until you feel happy with it. If in doubt, ask a colleague to help you. If they understand themselves they will be pleased to assist.

Tip 4: be numerate, be very numerate

Negotiations usually include financial implications. Get a good calculator and know how to handle it. Fumblers won't win friends, and certainly won't instil confidence in customers.

Be aware of the possibly dramatic effect that even a small price change has on profits (assuming volumes stay constant). A 10 per cent variance in sales revenue results in a 20 per cent change in net profit, because of the effect caused by the fixed costs, which stay constant, whatever the sales volume (see below).

Effects of price change on profit

		10% increase	10% decrease
Sales revenue	£50,000	£55,000	£45,000
Variable costs	£30,000	£33,000	£27,000
Gross profit	**£20,000**	**£22,000**	**£18,000**
Fixed costs	£10,000	£10,000	£10,000
Net profit	**£10,000**	**£12,000**	**£8,000**

A £5,000 increase in revenue equates to a £2,000 increase in profit. Compared with the normal profit margin of 20 per cent (based on sales of £50,000), the incremental £5,000 sales now brings in an additional £2,000 in profit (ie each additional pound brings in an additional 40p of profit).

Conversely, a £5,000 reduction in revenue means a £2,000 fall in profit (ie every one pound less revenue is harming profits by 40p).

'Many a man has busted in business because his tie didn't match his socks'

– Frank McKinney Husband

Tip 5: discount versus bonus

Discounts are price reductions. Bonuses are rewards for performance. Discounts are granted. Bonuses are earned.

The expectation of a bonus encourages the buyer to do more. A discount can become a regular commitment, eventually forming an implied agreed price. Once a discount is established, it is more difficult to eliminate it.

- A bonus maintains the base price.
- The bonus is a management instrument for achieving a large number of goals.
- A bonus can be based on total quantity.
- A bonus can be based on a quantity over and above a threshold.
- A bonus does not necessarily have to be monetary.
- There is no such thing as a bonus in advance.

Firmly reject unjustifiable demands for discounts at the outset, before they get out of hand.

Ask the customer to give a reason for his or her request for a discount and ask him or her to justify the level of demand being requested (politely and tactfully, of course).

Tip 6: the effect of a markdown on gross profit

The table below shows that when you discount you have to sell a lot more just to stay still, in terms of profitability. Of course, there are sometimes valid reasons for cutting your price – competition or need to move stock, for example. But it's worth seeing if there may be another way of achieving the same result before resorting to an expensive price reduction.

Increased amount that must be sold to retain existing levels of profit when prices are cut

If you cut	With present gross profit of:			
price by:	**10%**	**20%**	**30%**	**40%**
5%	100%	33.3%	20%	14.3%
10%	–	200%	50%	33.3%
15%	–	–	100%	60%
20%	–	–	200%	100%

For example, if your gross profit margin is 30 per cent and you discount by just 15 per cent, you will need to sell twice as much (100 per cent) to achieve the same margin as before you started discounting.

Try giving a 'free' offer, a baker's dozen, extra service, free delivery or added value, for example. You may find that the value of additional service is worth more to the customer than the price discount – and will cost you less.

'Work is life, and without it there's nothing but fear and insecurity'

– John Lennon

Tip 7: money talks

Back up your sales arguments by expressing the extra profit or increased savings you can offer to your customer in *specific money terms*. Just to say, 'This will save you money' is not powerful enough. A buyer will be more turned on by knowing exactly *how much* money he will be saving over *what period of time*.

You'll find the trouble taken to work out these specifics in advance of the meeting, such as the money saved over, say, a month-long period, will be worth it when it comes to negotiating a deal with the customer.

Tip 8: it's not just the price, you know

It's not just the price on the invoice that counts. There are several hidden aspects that affect the customer's buying decision. If your competitor sells a product for £100, and you offer an almost identical product for £80, you may be flummoxed when your rival still gets the order.

Why didn't you get the business? It could be to do with that retrospective discount the customer gets at the end of each quarter if he hits a certain turnover target. Or it could be that 'sales conference' for top customers in New York that he's in line for. It could be the competitor's national advertising campaign that is about to break. Or it could be the yearly 'loyalty bonus' that's due to be paid in only a couple of months' time.

Ask your customer why you didn't get the business *this time*, and what would enable you to get it *next time*. You may get a straight answer, and then at least you will know what will turn your customer on when you're planning your next promotion.

It may not simply be the price that has to be right.

'Statistics are no substitute for judgement'

– Henry Clay

Tip 9: moving into management

Well done! After a lot of hard graft as an area manager, you have been promoted to national or regional sales manager, with area managers now reporting to you. But don't let it go to your head. Do get to know key elements of your team's territory. Don't ever undermine your area manager with your presence and *never* suggest that if a customer has a problem they should now bypass the area manager and come directly to you.

Key information about your team's customers that you should get to know include:

- How many customers does your team have in total?
- How many does each area manager have?
- Where are they concentrated geographically?
- Who are their best customers by turnover and profitability?
- Can you identify your team's top 100, 50, 20 and 10 customers?

What can you do to support your area managers in their relationships with these customers? How about identifying each manager's top 10, and then visit those customers together? Let the customers know how much you and your company appreciate their business.

And by helping your area managers achieve their targets they are helping you to achieve your own.

Tip 10: people buy from people – so get to know them

The way you approach potential customers is going to be different according to the type of business you are in. For example, if you are selling into the FMCG market it may be appropriate (even expected, perhaps) to just 'call in', without an appointment, see the manager, and write out an order there and then.

Things are probably very different, however, in the case of selling capital goods, or high value 'one off' items, with contracts possibly worth hundreds of thousands of pounds. Your first visit will not usually bring you the desired order – that will come later, after you have established contact, and rapport, with the relevant personnel.

Work out a staged goal plan covering a set period of time, and start by gaining information about the prospective customer. Make contact with management, engineers and buyers and find out who is who, and who makes which decisions.

The more people you get to know in the process, the better. People still buy from people, so bothering to establish as many personal contacts as possible cannot be a bad thing, and you will reap rewards in the long run.

'Figures won't lie, but liars will figure'

– Charles H Grosvenor

Tip 11: be ready with your figures at the drop of a hat

It's all very well being able to sell but a good salesperson always knows *how much* he's sold. You never know when you might get a call from your MD asking for some information on your turnover figures so far this month, or this year or this quarter. Being aware of the past also helps you make decisions about the future.

He might also ask you to give a brief résumé of your sales territory, at a moment's notice, to a visiting VIP, and you can be sure he doesn't want waffle. Facts and figures are the name of the game so be constantly aware of details such as:

- where your territory is;
- how much annual turnover is achieved in total, and by your top 80 per cent of customers;
- how much has business increased or decreased over the previous year;
- which products or services are particularly important for your business, and why;
- any special considerations that particularly affect the business in your area;
- plans you have for business development.

You will be expected to know the basics about your business. You will get a chance to show off your professionalism if you are constantly prepared to give a 10-minute synopsis at the drop of a hat.

Tip 12: promises, promises

Have you ever experienced that feeling when you go into a meeting with a prospective customer, the meeting goes brilliantly, and you come out *absolutely certain* that you will get an order in due course.

You were sure that the price was right, the product just what the customer wanted, your delivery time was acceptable – and you got on so well, too. Without doubt the order was in the bag – it was as good as promised – or so you thought.

A week goes by, and no order comes. You phone, but can't get past the gatekeeper. For some reason everything has gone cold and you realize that the 'promise' of an order was in fact just an excuse for a total refusal.

Remember – an order is only an order when it's signed, sealed and delivered. Then it's yours.

'A salesman has got to dream, boy, it goes with the territory'

– Arthur Miller

Tip 13: watch out for the 'price:volume' tactic

When dealing with price negotiation, if there are variances in quantities beware that sometimes a buyer may deliberately add uncertainty as to the quantities needed.

He may well understate the quantity, while progressively revealing the real figure. For example: 'We will need 500 per week, what is the price?' When you respond, he then says: 'But if business goes well, we may need 600 per week. What would the price be then?' If you move on the original price, the buyer is establishing a price:volume ratio, and will expect further price reduction when moving toward the (true) quantity (which was known by him all along). 'So what further price reduction can you offer for 700 per week?' will be the next question just around the corner.

If you sense that a buyer is starting to lead you down this path, preempt him by offering a price:volume agreement up front. A response to the first question such as, 'Price breaks exist on quantities of 800 and 1,000, so we can achieve a better price if we can talk in terms of these volumes' will help you to retake command of the situation.

Ask open questions to determine as much information as possible, as information means power, and power often leads to successful negotiation, especially when it comes to price.

Geof the exec

Geof was disappointed with his 'case of drinks' prize from his company – but perhaps distinguishing 'profit' from 'turnover' might have helped

8

Healthy living – reducing stress and improving sales

A healthy lifestyle will cut the waistline and add to the bottom line

Selling is potentially one of the most stressful, unhealthy professions of them all. Salespeople constantly have to meet – and beat – targets. And no sooner is a target met than another, almost always bigger one, looms over the not-too-distant horizon. It never stops.

Couple the stresses and strains of escalating sales targets with a hectic lifestyle that often means long hours driving, snatching fast food on the go, getting caught in traffic jams, trouble parking, other travel delays, constantly making face-to-face presentations – the list is endless – and you have a potential recipe for disaster. It is no wonder that many salespeople burn out at a comparatively young age.

It is therefore vitally important for salespeople to do all they can to maintain a healthy lifestyle, and to keep stress levels to a minimum and stamina levels at a maximum. A healthy, unstressed salesperson will consistently outperform one who is not, and for a longer period of time.

In a recent survey conducted in *CoatHanger – The Sales Driver* magazine, over 90 per cent of salespeople admitted they were worried about living an unhealthy lifestyle, and that they would welcome help in making improvements.

In this chapter we aim to give a series of practical tips aimed at turning potential health and stress negatives into positives. They range from what you eat, and when you eat it, to regular exercise, to the art of positive thinking.

Eating the right food at the right time is of vital importance and is often underestimated. Certain foods help put you in a good sales mood whereas others can make you lethargic just when you need to be on top of your game. Diet also has a major effect on cholesterol levels, and when you consider that a third of all deaths from heart disease result from sedentary lifestyles prevalent in high-mileage drivers, then it all gets thrown into pretty sharp focus.

The correct level of exercise goes hand-in-hand with the right food. Too much can be bad for you, not enough is a lot worse. Non-stressful physical activity is a fantastic way to control weight, those deadly cholesterol levels, blood pressure, mood and stress, and to help delay the dreaded ageing process.

If you can get the diet/exercise equation right then lower stress levels and the ability to deal with that stress will follow suit. Salespeople who adopt a positive frame of mind are far less likely to suffer the damaging effects of stress and stress-related conditions.

Positive attitudes to change (which is one of the greatest causes of stress), deadlines, targets, customer and colleague relationships, and the like, will help you become healthier, wealthier and maybe even a little wiser. You will also sell more.

A word of warning. An excess of 'quick-fix' stimulants such as chocolate and caffeine doesn't work, at least not long term. So stay away from them, we say, and instead try an apple a day to keep stress at bay.

Oh no! Disaster story!

Continued from page 103 ...

'So what?' you might ask. When you are in a selling situation, remember to respect your customer's territory. It is his ground – not yours. When you are on your own turf then that's a different matter. But when you are making a visit to your customer don't make assumptions about what he thinks is acceptable behaviour. Your idea might be a lot different from theirs.

Of course it is only human to make mistakes, and it's true that nobody can be perfect all the time. But there are certain mistakes that can be avoided. So think twice about what you are doing, and remember what you were taught in your old physics lessons: every action creates an equal and opposite reaction.

'It's much easier to follow a pioneer than be a pioneer'

– Richard Branson

Tip 1: dashboard dining tips

- Start off your day with a decent breakfast. You don't want to be thinking of your stomach when you should be thinking of your sales strategy.
- Always eat something in the middle of the day. This keeps blood sugar up and stops you getting in a bad mood.
- Plump for medium carbohydrate foods such as a wholemeal sandwich filled with chicken or ham, plus salad. Wash down with a milkshake, mineral water or fruit juice.
- Avoid too much coffee and sugary things like sweets – they give an instant energy high, only to be followed by a dispiriting low when it is time for the sales call.
- Definitely avoid alcohol. OK, a pint of shandy or a spritzer should be within the limit, but they will make you as drowsy as hell and you won't feel like doing any work in the afternoon – horrible when you know you have to.
- Buy a car tidy. Empty crisp packets and drinks cans slung around the interior won't portray the right image to the customer or boss when they unexpectedly ask for a lift.
- Always keep a clean tablecloth and cutlery (for two) in the car. You never know when you might have a dashboard dining guest!

Tip 2: lazy salespeople wanted

- So lazy that they take advantage of every sales aid they can get their hands on.
- So lazy that they copy the methods of the most successful salespeople.
- So lazy that they carefully plan their routes to cut travelling time.
- So lazy that they concentrate their efforts on the customers and prospects that represent the most business.
- So lazy that they make appointments so as to avoid calling on customers who are unavailable.
- So lazy that they keep records on each customer and prospect so that they won't strain their memory.
- So lazy that they insist on getting a good night's sleep every night, especially during exhibition week.
- So lazy that they refuse to run errands for their spouse during work time.

'To err is human, but to really foul things up requires a computer'
– Philip Howard

Tip 3: listen 'ere

Listen to other people. Not just hear them, but *really listen* to them. Often what others say can be more important than what *you* say, so instead of immediately responding, just listen.

Listen to your own intuition and trust it. Being well-informed before making a decision is obviously beneficial, but quite often your gut feeling was the right one all along.

Listen out for questions. Only then offer advice or answers. Most people don't like to be force fed with advice that is not called for. But if you *are* asked for advice, you can then be sure of that person's undivided attention.

Listen to your doctor. If you are juggling family life with a career your health may easily get overlooked. So have a check-up on a regular basis (more frequently as you get older) because your health is your most valuable asset. Your boss won't thank you for being a hero workaholic if you then need six weeks off due to a *preventable* illness. And nor will your loved ones.

Tip 4: reducing nerves and tension before a presentation

That tense, nervous feeling has possibly been eliminated from those meetings you have with familiar, regular customers who have almost become personal friends that you can share a drink and a laugh with.

But how about that all-important presentation you've been working for ages to get? You've not met the customer before and you have to get it right, possibly in front of their colleagues (or perhaps even worse, your own sales director).

As well as the basics, such as researching where you're going and allowing *plenty* of time to get there (and parking, going through security, signing in at reception), there are also some simple physical exercises you can do to reduce those butterflies. But make sure you do these in private.

- Start by frowning, then squeeze your face as though it's being squashed between your chin and forehead.
- Stretch your mouth wide open and open your eyes as wide as possible.
- Close your eyes very tight, purse your lips and scrunch up your face as if it's being squashed sideways.
- Take a series of deep, controlled breaths through the nose, closing your eyes and exhaling through the mouth.
- Finally, give yourself a *big* smile.

'A bank is a place that will lend you money if you can prove you don't need it'

– Bob Hope

Tip 5: reduce stress – cut back on stimulants

Being in sales can be stressful enough without the added anxiety brought about from driving at speed in today's traffic. Add to that deadlines for reports required by the boss, promotional campaigns, sales targets, late deliveries, irate customers, and, and, and… all these things add pressure to go for 'quick-fix' stimulant solutions.

But excess coffee, cigarettes, chocolate and other sweets, overeating as well as too much alcohol after work may only help to overcome fatigue, anxiety and tension in the short term, and do no good whatsoever in the long term.

Taking stimulants like chocolate and coffee can also bring about headaches or insomnia, which in turn increase the stress due to tiredness. And then tiredness reduces your efficiency at work, resulting in your workload not being achieved, adding to more stress – and so the cycle goes on.

Break the cycle by taking a relaxing break, seeing a doctor if the headaches persist, cutting out caffeine and thinking about a hobby. Try taking Natracalm or Natrasleep tablets – non-habit-forming herbal remedies. They only cost a few pounds a packet (lasting about a month) and are available from most supermarkets.

Tip 6: make office meetings less of a pain in the neck

Office meetings are sometimes unavoidable, but unfortunately can also be a waste of time. If you are called to attend a meeting, make sure that:

- you are informed about when it will be, and allow yourself some time to prepare for it;
- you understand what the meeting will be about, and have enough information with you – have enough copies of relevant reports to hand round if necessary as it shows that you are well organized;
- you are punctual as being late is rude and wastes other people's time;
- you know beforehand how long the meeting is likely to last – if the meeting is digressing try to politely steer it back on course;
- someone is taking minutes – this should have already been arranged but, if not, offer to do it yourself;
- you see the positive things about having the meeting in the first place.

Make it your personal goal to get something out of the meeting that will directly help you. That way you won't think that it's all been a total pain in the you-know-what.

'Business neglected is business lost'

– Daniel Defoe

Tip 7: keep calm – five ways to help avoid stress

1. Start 10 minutes early. Not only will you avoid the stress of being late but, if all goes well, you'll have 10 minutes before your appointment to relax. But don't anticipate using the 10 minutes to *prepare* for the meeting – that should have been done earlier.
2. Try herbal tea. If each time you visit a customer you drink tea or coffee, your caffeine intake is adding to a stressful feeling. Invest in a packet of herbal tea that you ask your host to use for you and you may find your ability to remain calm is enhanced many times.
3. Don't worry about the future. Most worries are about what might happen in the future, but in most cases they actually don't happen. Concentrate on the present and you'll find that the future takes care of itself.
4. Turn the music off. When driving a long distance, especially on the motorway, try turning off the car stereo a few miles before arriving at your destination. The relief to your ears will calm the mind.
5. Spending too early. Don't spend that commission before you've got it – wait for the payment to go into the bank first and *then* reward yourself. The last thing you want to project to customers is how much you *need* that order.

Tip 8: change

Some people like to blame their problems on the changes that are going on around them, but in fact it's the *resistance* to change that causes the most stress. Don't waste emotional energy trying to hang on to old habits but embrace changes openly. People may not be able to control what the changes are but they can control how they react to them.

'There's three things you can predict in life: tax, death and more meetings'

– Mike Moore

Tip 9: four ways to improve your day

1. Wear sensible, well fitting shoes. Your business meeting will be less successful if you are constantly thinking about how much your feet are killing you. And if you have to drive a long distance to your appointment, try wearing a pair of more relaxing 'slippers' on the journey. But don't forget to change them again before going into the meeting.
2. Say 'no'. Your efficiency and state of mind will be affected if you are overloaded with work. It can sometimes be harder to say 'no' than 'yes' to new requests but half the battle is to recognize just how much you are capable of doing. Then you can politely but firmly turn down – or reschedule – new tasks.
3. Set your own agenda. You will have more time to relax and be calm if you don't allow others to dictate your pace too much.
4. Make friends and keep them. Common deathbed regrets relate to neglected relationships – not unfinished business. It's people that make business so if you tend to get too serious over work, remind yourself that it could all be over tomorrow – and smile along the way.

Tip 10: get organized – go home on Friday afternoon

No, we're not suggesting for sales drivers to put their feet up watching *Home and Away*, but to set aside some time each week to get administration and paperwork bang up to date. Friday afternoon is a good time, especially as many customers are away themselves and may not particularly appreciate a sales call anyway.

As well as catching up on paperwork, plan out your following week so that you know where you're meant to be and when. Use your afternoon to keep abreast of developments in your industry, and company. Refresh your product knowledge by reading trade journals, and familiarize yourself with new brochures from competitors.

And don't worry about scornful remarks from others like, 'Oh yeah, he's got the afternoon off again'. You don't *have* to be hurtling down the motorway, or be in front of a customer, to be productive. By going home you will be more efficient on Monday morning if you clear your workload, and your mind, on Friday afternoon.

Set up your homework space separate from living or sleeping areas, so that you can switch off and leave work behind at the end of the day. If space is tight, consider buying a shed and turning that into your own office. Insulation, a small desk and filing cabinet, plus a separate phone line can be installed for a couple of hundred pounds.

'Corruption is simply business without scruples'

– Anon

Tip 11: put your feet up

We're all human. No one can keep going 100 per cent all the time. Have you ever felt absolutely worn out, stressed, drained of all energy, with no desire to do anything at all? Well, in that case don't do anything. Stop everything. Put your feet up, and do nothing – no phone calls, no talking, no listening, no meetings, and not even any thinking. If you are in an office, shut the door to indicate you are not to be disturbed. If you don't have the luxury of your own office, go outside to the car. Colleagues will hopefully be approving and would themselves probably benefit from trying it as well.

This is different from 'power napping', which is all the rage for top-ranking corporates in the States and Japan. How anyone can instantly go to sleep for fifteen minutes and then suddenly wake up again and carry on is a mystery. No, this is more of a simple relaxation practice to rejuvenate the muscles and brain cells.

Forget about the time and sit completely still for as long as it takes before you get the urge to start moving again. When we say 'put your feet up', that isn't necessarily meant in the literal sense, unless you can get into the back of your car. Don't move again until you really feel restless.

You'll often find that your energy levels will have been restored after no more than fifteen minutes and you'll be twice as efficient as you were before and raring to pick up where you left off.

Tip 12: failure (non-success) can be positive

Failure in achieving something you've set out to do needn't be seen by you or anyone else as negative. Non-success – not failure – will probably occur at least twice a day and its occurrence is less important than what your attitude is towards it:

- See non-success as a learning experience. Work out why things didn't go according to plan, and improve upon them for next time – then move on.
- See non-success as the feedback needed in order to change direction. If your customer loves everything you do, but still doesn't buy, you've got nowhere to turn.
- See non-success as a way to have a good laugh. You might have wanted the ground to swallow you up during that disastrous sales meeting but seeing the funny side will help to heal your wounds. Embellish the story for others to laugh with you. You have to have a sense of humour to survive in sales!
- See non-success as a practice run. Even if you make a tip-top presentation, but you still don't get the order, just be thankful that you'd been given a chance to practise and perfect your selling skills.
- See non-success as part of the sales numbers game. See more people, more often and you'll get more rejection – but also you'll get more sales and make more money. It's not the number of times you fail that counts, but the number of times you succeed.

'One company's research is another's development'

– Anon

Tip 13: credit where it's due – and be fair about it

Many companies operate an annual appraisal system for everyone within the organization. If yours doesn't, it may be a good idea to suggest one as an appraisal presents a golden opportunity to really find out a number of things.

Personal and business objectives can be discussed, and appraisals can often lead to performance improvements, providing they are conducted with the four 'F's – *Frequent, Fulsome, Feedback* and *Fair*.

Make sure that the *frequency* of the appraisal is known to all – and stick to your schedule.

Fulsome refers to the scope of the appraisal. Cover all aspects, including quality of work and general attitude. Give praise where it's due, so long as it is sincere and warranted.

Appraisals should be motivational – otherwise what's the point? If you are the boss, how about asking your staff to appraise you? *Feedback* should flow in both directions, after all.

Fairness is critical to both parties, the appraiser and the appraisee. If there is the slightest suspicion that anything is seeming unfair, ask directly about it and clear it up before moving on.

Geof the exec

Geof was upset about being second best to an executive toy – but perhaps he could have also done with some stress relief himself

9

And finally...

So now you have read *Bite-Size Sales Tips* – unless of course you are one of those people who start a book at the back! If you are one of those types, then can we politely suggest you take a good look at the book before you carry on reading this message.

OK. Those of you still with us, we hope you have enjoyed (or will enjoy) this book, and that it will become a valuable companion to you for the rest of your career as a sales professional.

We have designed the book to be there by your side at all times, no matter what sales situation you find yourself in. No single book can cover every eventuality, but we are confident that you will find inspiration from at least one of our bite size sales tips wherever you are and whoever you are dealing with.

Say, for example, that you are waiting in the reception area to see one of your most important customers. Simply turn to the 'Customers – how to give them what they want' section, and you should find something there that will inspire you to maximize the sale.

Say, for example, you are planning a heavy week on the road, at the sharp end. Then what could be better than referring to the 'On the road – practical ideas on getting to your customer' section for a host of tips in making the best of your time?

Say, for example, that you have a key sales presentation to make –

the one that could make or break the deal. For guaranteed success all you need to do is locate the 'Presenting your case – putting across the right message' section.

Say, for example, you are new to sales (or have been in sales for 30 years for that matter) and you want to make sure you are getting the basic skills right. All you have to do is go to the 'Just starting out – basic selling tips' section and you will be on the right track.

Say for example, you are feeling stressed out, and wondering how you are going to cope with the demands being placed on you. Just turn to the 'Healthy Living – reducing stress and improving sales' section, and you will see light at the end of the tunnel.

And say, for example, you are about to enter into some tough negotiations with a key potential customer. Flick through to the 'Negotiation – the skill in selling' section and you will go into that meeting with the confidence that will give you the edge.

Finally, may we wish you success upon success in the daunting yet exciting, demanding yet rewarding, frustrating yet inspiring sales profession. Our hope is that this book will help you achieve and maintain that success.

Neil Watson and Steve Hurst